★ ★ ★ ★ ★ ★ ★ ★ ★ ★ ★ ★ ★ ★ ★ ★ ★

# We the People

★ ★ ★ ★ ★ ★ ★ ★ ★ ★ ★ ★ ★ ★ ★ ★

# We the People

## RICHARD C. HALVERSON
*Chaplain, United States Senate*

**Regal Books**

A Division of GL Publications
Ventura, California, U.S.A.

Published by Regal Books
A Division of GL Publications
Ventura, California 93006
Printed in U.S.A.

Scripture quotations in this publication are from:
The HOLY BIBLE: NEW INTERNATIONAL VERSION. Copyright © 1973, 1978, 1984
by the International Bible Society. Used by permission of Zondervan Bible Publishers.

**Library of Congress Cataloging in Publication Data**

Halverson, Richard C.
   We the people.

   Bibliography: p.
   1. Political participation—United States. 2. Christians—United States—Political
activity. 3. Christianity and politics. I. Title.
JK1764.H35    1987                323′042′0973                87-4804
ISBN 0-8307-1220-8

Any omission of credits or permissions granted is unintentional. The publisher requests
documentation for future printings.

Rights for publishing this book in other languages are contracted by Gospel Literature
International (GLINT) foundation. GLINT also provides technical help for the
adaptation, translation, and publishing of Bible study resources and books in scores of
languages worldwide. For further information, contact GLINT, Post Office Box 488,
Rosemead, California, 91770, U.S.A., or the publisher.

★ ★ ★ ★ ★ ★ ★ ★ ★ ★ ★ ★ ★ ★ ★ ★ ★ ★

*"Virtually every other revolution in history just exchanged one set of rulers for another. Our revolution is the first to say the people are the masters and government is their servant."*

—— RONALD REAGAN ——
President of the United States

# Dedication

To Senator Mark Hatfield and his lovely lady, Antoinette, whose friendship since the early '50s has meant more to me than words can express, and whose leadership and inspiration have been of incalculable value to the people of God, the nation and the world.

# Acknowledgments

Producing this manuscript would have been impossible were it not for the efficient, accurate work of Mrs. Joan Crownover, who patiently typed the several drafts necessary to complete it. Her incredible speed and accuracy, together with a wonderfully cooperative attitude, were indispensable contributions. And I appreciate so much the help of Bill St. Cyr, beloved friend and partner in the office, who responded instantly and thoroughly when research was needed. These two fine friends made the job much easier and I thank God for them.

# We the People

of the United States, in order to form a more perfect Union, establish Justice, insure domestic Tranquility, provide for the common defence, promote the general Welfare, and secure the Blessings of Liberty to ourselves and our Posterity, do ordain and establish this Constitution for the United States of America.

## Article. I.

Section. 1. All legislative Powers herein granted shall be vested in a Congress of the United States, which shall consist of a Senate and House of Representatives.

Section. 2. The House of Representatives shall be composed of Members chosen every second Year by the People of the several States, and the Electors in each State shall have the Qualifications requisite for Electors of the most numerous Branch of the State Legislature.

No Person shall be a Representative who shall not have attained to the Age of twenty five Years, and been seven Years a Citizen of the United States, and who shall not, when elected, be an Inhabitant of that State in which he shall be chosen.

Representatives and direct Taxes shall be apportioned among the several States which may be included within this Union, according to their respective Numbers, which shall be determined by adding to the whole Number of free Persons, including those bound to Service for a Term of Years, and excluding Indians not taxed, three fifths of all other Persons. The actual Enumeration shall be made within three Years after the first Meeting of the Congress of the United States, and within every subsequent Term of ten Years, in such Manner as they shall by Law direct. The Number of Representatives shall not exceed one for every thirty Thousand, but each State shall have at Least one Representative; and until such enumeration shall be made, the State of New Hampshire shall be entitled to chuse three, Massachusetts eight, Rhode Island and Providence Plantations one, Connecticut five, New York six, New Jersey four, Pennsylvania eight, Delaware one, Maryland six, Virginia ten, North Carolina five, South Carolina five, and Georgia three.

When vacancies happen in the Representation from any State, the Executive Authority thereof shall issue Writs of Election to fill such Vacancies.

The House of Representatives shall chuse their Speaker and other Officers; and shall have the sole Power of Impeachment.

Section. 3. The Senate of the United States shall be composed of two Senators from each State, chosen by the Legislature thereof, for six Years; and each Senator shall have one Vote.

Immediately after they shall be assembled in Consequence of the first Election, they shall be divided as equally as may be into three Classes. The Seats of the Senators of the first Class shall be vacated at the Expiration of the second Year, of the second Class at the Expiration of the fourth Year, and of the third Class at the Expiration of the sixth Year, so that one third may be chosen every second Year; and if Vacancies happen by Resignation, or otherwise, during the Recess of the Legislature of any State, the Executive thereof may make temporary Appointments until the next Meeting of the Legislature, which shall then fill such Vacancies.

No Person shall be a Senator who shall not have attained to the Age of thirty Years, and been nine Years a Citizen of the United States, and who shall not, when elected, be an Inhabitant of that State for which he shall be chosen.

The Vice President of the United States shall be President of the Senate, but shall have no Vote, unless they be equally divided.

The Senate shall chuse their other Officers, and also a President pro tempore, in the Absence of the Vice President, or when he shall exercise the Office of President of the United States.

The Senate shall have the sole Power to try all Impeachments. When sitting for that Purpose, they shall be on Oath or Affirmation. When the President of the United States is tried, the Chief Justice shall preside: And no Person shall be convicted without the Concurrence of two thirds of the Members present.

Judgment in Cases of Impeachment shall not extend further than to removal from Office, and disqualification to hold and enjoy any Office of honor, Trust or Profit under the United States: but the Party convicted shall nevertheless be liable and subject to Indictment, Trial, Judgment and Punishment, according to Law.

Section. 4. The Times, Places and Manner of holding Elections for Senators and Representatives, shall be prescribed in each State by the Legislature thereof; but the Congress may at any time by Law make or alter such Regulations, except as to the Places of chusing Senators.

The Congress shall assemble at least once in every Year, and such Meeting shall be on the first Monday in December, unless they shall by Law appoint a different Day.

Section. 5. Each House shall be the Judge of the Elections, Returns and Qualifications of its own Members, and a Majority of each shall constitute a Quorum to do Business; but a smaller Number may adjourn from day to day, and may be authorized to compel the Attendance of absent Members, in such Manner, and under such Penalties as each House may provide.

Each House may determine the Rules of its Proceedings, punish its Members for disorderly Behaviour, and, with the Concurrence of two thirds, expel a Member.

Each House shall keep a Journal of its Proceedings, and from time to time publish the same, excepting such Parts as may in their Judgment require Secrecy; and the Yeas and Nays of the Members of either House on any question shall, at the Desire of one fifth of those Present, be entered on the Journal.

Neither House, during the Session of Congress, shall, without the Consent of the other, adjourn for more than three days, nor to any other Place than that in which the two Houses shall be sitting.

Section. 6. The Senators and Representatives shall receive a Compensation for their Services, to be ascertained by Law, and paid out of the Treasury of the United States. They shall in all Cases, except Treason, Felony and Breach of the Peace, be privileged from Arrest during their Attendance at the Session of their respective Houses, and in going to and returning from the same; and for any Speech or Debate in either House, they shall not be questioned in any other Place.

No Senator or Representative shall, during the Time for which he was elected, be appointed to any civil Office under the Authority of the United States, which shall have been created, or the Emoluments whereof shall have been encreased during such time; and no Person holding any Office under the United States, shall be a Member of either House during his Continuance in Office.

Section. 7. All Bills for raising Revenue shall originate in the House of Representatives; but the Senate may propose or concur with Amendments as on other Bills.

Every Bill which shall have passed the House of Representatives and the Senate, shall, before it become a Law, be presented to the President of the

"We, the People of the United States, in Order to form a more perfect Union, establish Justice, insure domestic Tranquility, provide for the common defense, promote the general Welfare, and secure the Blessings of Liberty to ourselves and our Posterity do ordain and establish this Constitution for the United States of America."

Preamble to the Constitution of the United States

---

*God of our fathers, these words are so familiar that we hear them with a yawn. Help us to realize how revolutionary—how radical—they must have sounded at a time when governments were sovereign and people were subjects. As we approach the bicentennial of the Constitution, awaken the people to the unprecedented political system which is our legacy and renew them in their understanding and commitment. Help them to comprehend that in this system the people are sovereign and the government receives its just powers from their consent. Help the people to recognize that the system breaks down when they abdicate their sovereignty. Forgive the false thinking of the people as "us" and the government as "them." Gracious God, may November fourth and the time between now and then see the renewal of the people in taking their sovereignty as seriously as the Senate does. In the name of Him Who is Lord of history,*
*Amen.*

Prayer in the Senate—July 17, 1986

# Contents

# Introduction

**T**hirty years in Washington, D.C., two and a half of them solely with the Prayer Breakfast Movement, twenty-two and a half as pastor of Fourth Presbyterian Church, and the past five as chaplain of the United States Senate, have taught me many things, my former ignorance of which I've come to realize only recently.

As an associate in the Prayer Breakfast Movement, I was introduced to the Senate and House prayer breakfasts, which occur weekly when Congress is in session, and I have been honored to attend those prayer breakfasts on a regular basis for 30 years. Though senators and representatives alone are invited to lead these prayer breakfasts, it has been a privilege for me to be involved in the table conversation before the message. It has also been a way to get acquainted with members of Congress and to find out how they think and feel about their lives, their public trust, and their commitment to Jesus Christ.

In addition, I have been able to participate in many of the prayer breakfast groups, which meet in nearly every department of government, mostly on a weekly basis, some every other week, and a few monthly. This includes a monthly prayer breakfast that is attended by the judges of most of the courts in Washington, D.C., including two or three justices from the Supreme Court.

Almost invariably the discussions at these prayer breakfasts involve the relationship of religion to public life or, in more recent years, the relevance of Jesus Christ and His gospel to the lives of men and women in public service. Not uncommonly the leaders of the group include in their messages a personal witness to the relevance of their own faith and the responsibility they bear in their positions.

The work of a pastor in the nation's capital is unique in the sense that he is made aware, in one way or another, of nearly every issue that involves the nation as well as the world. The Washington pastor is also informed of most of the movements of churches or various religious groups regarding protests or demonstrations planned in the city. Though not always, he is generally given the details and usually invited to be involved to some extent.

My pastorate at the Fourth Presbyterian Church covered the entire period of the Civil Rights Movement and the Vietnam War. The National Capitol Union Presbytery during those years had a very strong and articulate social action committee. Social activism dominated much of the debate in our presbytery meetings held 10 months out of the year. I believe it is safe to say that a Washington pastor has a perspective on most of these national and world issues that pastors in other cities may not have—at least not to the same degree.

In addition to the protests and demonstrations, the chaplains of the House and Senate often find themselves in the vortex of the issues that confront the Congress, especially those impinging on religion or morality. My ministry as chaplain of the Senate has covered the school prayer debate, the abortion debate, and the exceedingly active and controversial church/state debate before, during and since the 1984 elections.

Since coming to Washington in 1956, it has been my privilege to visit most of the states and to speak to churches and church groups throughout the country. A period for questions usually follows and I do my best to answer, always reserving the right to say, "I don't know." I might add that a pastor from Washington, D.C., is assumed to know a great deal more than he really does about national and world affairs and, as can be imagined, it is assumed that the chaplain of the Senate knows a great deal more than he really does about the operation of government.

At this point I would like to insert a simple, but important disclaimer. It ought to be understood that I do not come to the task of writing this manuscript with any sense of expertise. The position I have the privilege to hold as chaplain of the Senate does not qualify me as a specialist in government. Actually, these years in the Senate have been, in that respect, a mixed blessing. I suppose there has been as much confusion as there has been insight and enlightenment. In the past few years there has been a movement on the part of the leadership and the members to examine the rules, the procedures, the precedents, and the traditions of the Senate in the hope that the Senate could be made to operate more effectively and efficiently.

Coming to Washington, almost totally ignorant of the operation of our government apart from a few facts remembered from civics and government classes in school, I have learned a great deal, though I must confess that I still feel naive when it comes to speaking on these matters. In fact, the concern rising out of my ignorance has been growing and deepening as I have discovered a like ignorance and naiveté, sometimes even cynicism, on the part of many people in the United States. This is doubly serious to me because most of my connections have been with people in the church or with various evangelical religious groups who not only should be knowledgeable of the affairs of government, but actually ought to be more involved than the average citizen.

This book might not have been written were it not for the fact that the leaders of the Presbyterian Congress on Renewal held in Dallas, Texas, January 1985, invited me to lead a workshop on the influence of public policy. Though I did not feel qualified to lead such a workshop, I was willing to take the risk, and prepared myself to the extent I could in anticipation of the opportunity. After my remarks the workshop was opened to questions from the audience, which I attempted to do my best to answer. The appendix of this book contains those questions and answers.

My impression is that the ignorance and cynicism concerning our political system and how it operates is the result of what I call, "thinking in categories and caricatures." In our culture today it seems most of us think of others in terms of a category, and the image of the category is a caricature drawn by a clever cartoonist. Whenever we think of that category we think of that caricature, which is our perception of a particular person, whether that person be a politician, a doctor, a lawyer, a clergyman, etc.

It has been my experience, since serving in the Senate, that the reality I experience every day is antithetical to the image reflected in conversation with many people I have spent time with over the past few years. Therefore I come to this very challenging task, not as an authority or an expert, but as a concerned citizen with a degree of experience, attempting to look at public life or government from a biblical perspective.

At the time of this writing, as we approach the 100th Congress, which will convene in January 1987, and the celebration of the bicentennial of the Constitution of the United States, it is expedient, indeed, imperative, that we who take our citizenship seriously should attempt to understand with greater clarity the political system that is such an incredible legacy from our forbears.

CHAPTER 1

# We the People

"We the People of the United States, in Order to form a more perfect Union, establish Justice, insure domestic Tranquility, provide for the common defence, promote the general Welfare, and secure the Blessings of Liberty to ourselves and our Posterity, do ordain and establish this Constitution for the United States of America."

"We, the people of the United States . . . do ordain and establish . . . " Try to imagine how these words must have sounded when monarchs were sovereign and people were subjects; when kings ruled by divine right; when thrones were ascended by royal progeny and people were "commoners." It is simply impossible to exaggerate how revolutionary this idea was 200 years ago.

Where did such a radical idea originate? Two sentences in the Declaration of Independence lay the foundation for this radical concept of human government. "We hold these truths to be self-evident, that all men are created equal, that they are endowed by

*"Signing of the Declaration of Independence, July 4, 1776, in Independence Hall, Philadelphia." The painting by John Trumbull shows John Adams, Roger Sherman, Robert Livingston, Thomas Jefferson and Benjamin Franklin presenting the proposed Declaration of Independence to the president of the Second Continental Congress.*

their Creator with certain unalienable Rights, that among these are Life, Liberty and the pursuit of Happiness. That to secure these rights, Governments are instituted among Men, deriving their just powers from the consent of the governed."

Think for a moment about these words that are fundamental to all we hold significant and precious in our public life. Think of this incredible statement in its various parts: "We hold these truths to be self-evident . . . " In other words, these truths are obvious and indisputable. "That all men are created equal . . . " Tragically, even many of our founding fathers who committed themselves, their lives, their sacred honor to this concept failed to live up to it. The United States is still recovering from this failure.

It is obvious, although not always recognized, that our forbears were not referring to equality in terms of personal size, shape, stamina, or talent when they referred to all men as being created equal. We are not all equal physically or emotionally or intellectually, in talent, capacity or aptitude. But we are all equal in terms of the next statement: "They are endowed by their Creator with certain unalienable Rights . . . "

Human rights are endowed by God, not by governments; that is what makes those rights inalienable. Inalienable means that they are incapable of being alienated, surrendered, or transferred; they are absolute, positive, unchallengeable, inviolable, sacrosanct. "Among these are Life, Liberty and the pursuit of Happiness."

Life—the right to live. God is the Author of life. Life comes from Him. Life is His to give. In fact, as one thinks more clearly about the biblical view of life, one realizes that God's life is the only life there is, and God has given His life to men.

In the second chapter of Genesis it is recorded that God shaped the human body from the dust of the ground and it was lifeless (see v. 7). Then Scripture records, "God . . . breathed into his nostrils the breath of life, and the man became a living being." The word *breath* is the same in the Hebrew as the word for spirit, so it can be paraphrased, God gave to man—lifeless man—His spirit.

*Our founding fathers committed themselves, their lives and their
sacred honor to the concepts of freedom on which our country is
founded. Tragically, many lives were lost in this stand for freedom.
On January 3, 1777, General Washington won an important victory
at the Battle of Princeton in New Jersey. Unfortunately, both sides
suffered heavy losses during the battle.*

When our first parents (Adam and Eve), as recorded in Genesis 3, believed the deception of the serpent rather than God's command, when they accepted the falsehood rather than the truth and followed the implications of that falsehood in disobeying God, they surrendered the life that God had given them, for God had said, "When you eat of it you will surely die" (Genesis 2:17). God had created us to live forever, His eternal life indwelling our bodies. In their rebellion, our first parents forfeited the eternal life of God in exchange for transiency, or temporal life, and passed the consequence of that rebellion on to the entire human family.

Eternal life, the gift of God, is restored when one is born again, born of God, born from above. When one believes in Jesus Christ, or receives Him into one's heart, then God's Holy Spirit again enters the human body, and that one who was eternally dead becomes eternally alive. The life that was lost in the Garden of Eden is restored through response to the gift of life through Jesus Christ, God's Son, our Saviour.

Liberty—what a great word—and how rare throughout human history! As our founding fathers understood it, there was little of it in their experience; next to life itself, it was their greatest treasure. One can perceive liberty in at least two different ways, giving it absolute value as some do, and relative value as do others. Well known is the strong declaration of Patrick Henry during a very eloquent speech in the formative days of our nation when he said, "As for me, give me liberty or give me death!" Without liberty life was meaningless to Patrick Henry, and there are many who still hold this view.

How can one adequately measure the divinely endowed gift of liberty? In His sovereign wisdom, God chose to create man (male/female) in His image with the power of choice. Endless discussion and debate have revolved around this rare right, which is basic to human history. Free choice exercises itself very early in childhood, and there is not a parent who has not struggled with this inevitable issue. All of the adjustments that life requires as child, parent, wife, husband, friend, employee, employer, partner, etc.,

*Before the Virginia Assembly, convened at Richmond, March 23, 1775, Patrick Henry delivered his most famous speech on the rights of the colonies concluding with, "Why stand we here idle? What is it that gentlemen wish? What would they have? Is life so dear, or peace so sweet, as to be purchased at the price of chains and slavery? Forbid it, Almighty God! I know not what course others may take, but as for me, give me liberty, or give me death."*

Photo from the archives of the Library of Congress

can be reduced to this basic reality. Choice is the inescapable issue in the battleground of all human relationships from birth to death. Choice is implicit in all legislation, and at the heart of every political system. In a sense, debate is no longer necessary once this issue—who chooses, who decides—is resolved.

The fundamental importance of choice, or decision, cannot be exaggerated. It was the Creator God's mandate. He created humans with freedom of choice, and it is safe to say that God knew how that freedom would be abused and the terrible consequences of that abuse throughout human history.

The pursuit of happiness—an interesting concept. Happiness is not guaranteed, but the right to pursue it is. This phrase gives us an insight into our founding fathers' understanding of equality. Humans are not equal in size or shape, in looks or talents or abilities, but God has given to each of us equal opportunity to persevere in the struggle in life in order to fulfill his or her full potential as a person. Any act by man or by law that violates this right contradicts our founding fathers' conviction about inalienable rights.

One of the hard realities to accept concerning the early days of our nation was the attitude toward slavery. Certainly this was a direct contradiction of their profession and their theory on human rights. It is an indication of a strange blankness or inconsistency or hardness of heart, of which human nature can be guilty. Unfortunately, we still have a long way to go to fulfill our founding fathers' dream of guaranteed human rights to all people.

Where do we start? How do we begin to find our way toward fulfilling that dream of guaranteed human rights? How can we, in seeking to attain rights for all people—even a minority of one—avoid the trap of serving isolated special interest groups, rather than achieving equal rights for all citizens in all walks of life, which was the original intent of the authors of the Constitution? How do we balance special interests for certain groups of people with people interests, which affect everyone?

Special interests are not always and invariably in competition with people interests; however, the fact is that special interests are usually in the interests of the people involved in groups, such as labor unions, for example. While in a conversation with a business executive in South Carolina, he remarked to me, "This PAC [Political Action Committee] represents the people, the people support it, and people are involved in its activities; it truly represents the people." He went on to say that many of the employees of his corporation who were previously uninvolved in the political process had been awakened and motivated and, because of their political action committee, were much involved in the political process. He knew of other political action committees of which this was also the case.

But the fact is there is potential for destructive division between special interests and people interests, which is aggravated if the people abdicate their sovereignty—if they are apathetic or indifferent to the political process. The problem has two sides. First, there is the emergence, strengthening and hardening of bureaucratization, control of any organization, civil, private or religious. The bureaucrats have their own convictions and their own concerns, their own policies and their own plans. And if the people allow it, these bureaucrats may, and sometimes do, use their power to influence legislation that represents their own interests rather than a particular concern of the people.

The other side of the problem arises when the private citizen, for whatever reason, loses interest in the political process, participating less and less, even at the polls, and, except when a bill or a law directly affects him (especially in an economic way), he withdraws and becomes totally uninvolved as a citizen.

This can also happen in a church denomination where men and women with special talents gravitate toward the administrative positions. Their job descriptions in the church often require them to be involved in the legislative process on issues of government that can sometimes impinge upon their denomination. In carrying out the work to which they are committed in their church, they must be well informed as to what is happening in Congress as well as in the White House.

The church administrator thus becomes increasingly informed and sophisticated about public service, legislation, executive and judicial activity, while at the same time the members of the local congregation, who fail to take the time or make the effort to get involved, become less and less informed. As a result, the bureaucrats in the religious institution make decisions at highest levels, bringing their influence to bear on the political process. The gap widens between denominational leaders and members of local churches until there is no communication at all, and the ecclesiastical officials less and less represent the will of the people.

The Washington Lobbyists and Lawyers Directory lists 9,500 lobbyists, 4,000 of whom are registered under the 1946 Lobby Registration Act. The number of political action committees registered with the Federal Election Commission as of July 14, 1986, was 4,092. The number of political action committees registered with the District of Columbia Board of Elections is 136.

These political action committees and lobbyists are a legitimate source of information and intelligence to the Members of Congress. They maintain a constant contact with the staff member of the senator or the representative whose job involves the interests of that particular lobbyist or political action committee. They are professional, knowledgeable and winsome, and they spend time attempting to influence legislation in the interests of the organizations they represent. It is a rare exception when a lobbyist uses underhanded methods, whether it has to do with money or morals, to get the results desired by the organization he represents. Lobbying is an honorable profession in the democratic process.

In the September 1986 issue of *U.S. News and World Report,* on the page entitled "Washington Whispers," there is a very interesting paragraph related to the tax reform bill: "Washington lobbyists admit defeat on tax reform, but that doesn't mean they're quitting. High-powered consultants are working already to shape transition rules, giving clients a break as the new rules phase into effect. Next, they'll draft technical corrections to restore still more loopholes in 1987."[1]

Here is a relentless presence in Washington, D.C. In state capitals as well as in county courthouses and city halls, representatives of special interests with professional expertise are doing everything in their power to influence government in the interests of their clients. If people presence is absent or minimal, it does not take a prophet to predict what interests will prevail.

This is a political reality in the United States and, on balance, it is constructive; but if the people do not exercise their power individually and collectively their interests are bound to be neglected. When that happens, the people will have no one to blame but themselves.

The basic necessity of people sovereignty is dramatized by the words of Romuald Spasowski, who has been called the "highest-ranking Communist official ever to defect to the west." Mr. Spasowski, in the epilogue to his book, *The Liberation of One,* wrote:

"Four years have passed since I raised my voice in protest, but the war declared on the Polish people continues.

"This war has no equal in history: on one side, a nation of nearly forty million people, and, on the other, a handful of reprobate Communists whose power is based solely in the police. Under normal circumstances, the nation would sweep that handful away—even the police would renounce them. But the circumstances are not normal. The handful are backed by Moscow. It is Moscow that assures the handful impunity and enables them to propagate the myth that People's Poland is an autonomous country; that there is a parliament, an executive branch, a judiciary, that parliament passes or repeals laws in accordance with the constitution; that the government uses the power granted to it; that there is law and order. It is a lie. The parliament represents no one, the handful receive their instructions directly from Moscow, and the courts carry out orders from the secret police. The situation in Poland confirms once again that Communists are morally bankrupt, that they would rather see a nation annihilated than see power slip from their hands."[2]

*Infinite God, we thank you for the political legacy our founding fathers gave us—for the incomparable system in the Constitution to preserve justice, truth and freedom. Forgive us for our impatience when we expect the efficiency of a dictatorship, while we demand the liberty of a democracy. Thank you, Lord, for the God-given pluralism that draws people of every race, creed and culture to this land of unprecedented opportunity. Preserve us, Lord, that pluralism will not polarize, that our diversity will not divide, that we will not allow controversy to be reduced to calamity. Grant the wisdom and grace that guided our forbears that we may continue to perfect, not plunder, the instruments of government that their vision produced. To the glory of your name,*
*Amen.*

Prayer in the Senate, February 5, 1986

# CHAPTER 2

# People Power

**W**hatever else results from the celebration of the bicentennial of the Constitution, we should see a recovery of the people's interest in and awareness of this indispensable foundation for our political system and their fresh commitment to the serious exercise of popular sovereignty or people power.

Assuming this renewal of interest, awareness and commitment to people responsibility, what are the ways people sovereignty is to be exercised? What conditions must an individual citizen expect to meet if he is to be faithful to the simple requirements our political system demands of the individual person?

Certainly the first requirement is to understand the system in its basic outline. This may seem elementary but contact with people throughout the nation these past few years indicates there is a great lack of appreciation for the political process by which our government operates. Perhaps ignorance is too strong a word, but certainly indifference would fit.

On many occasions the chaplain of the Senate has the opportunity to meet with people who visit the nation's capital. This may be at the request of a senator who is having a group of constituents come to the city, or it may be at the request of some citizen or student organization outside of the city who is bringing small groups to visit the nation's capital. They are always interested in the view of the Senate chaplain. Most often this meeting involves simply responding to questions with the understanding that the chaplain is not an expert in the political system but that he has impressions and has made observations.

Surprisingly, one of the first questions asked is, "How does a senator get to be a senator?" This may seem hard to believe, but the fact is that, not uncommonly, there are those who have the idea that the senators are appointed by the president. Many, incidentally, think the Capitol Building is the White House. I have learned never to be surprised at questions that betray almost total absence of understanding of how the political system or the government of the United States operates.

One form this betrayal of ignorance takes is a critical or sometimes even cynical remark. For example, a remark I have heard hundreds of times since I have been chaplain of the Senate is, "He is just doing that to get elected."

My response to this statement is to ask the person to think about what he has just said. Of course he is doing that to get elected. But who elects him? How does he get elected? What is the process whereby he becomes a member of the United States Senate?

He must be elected by the people. There is no other way that a person can become a senator. He is totally dependent upon the people's choice. This is what a political campaign is all about. And it is not only during a campaign—a senator is never free to ignore the people. He is unceasingly aware of the necessity of being in touch with them, of knowing what they think. He maintains a staff whose task is to help him stay aware and informed. Six years between elections may afford a degree of insulation, but with modern press and media bringing instant information, sensitivity to the people is imperative.

There is, of course, a cynical implication to this statement, namely that speeches are simply rhetoric—that it will make no dif-

*Our country is made up of people from all races, religions and creeds, people who work in different jobs, at different levels. Each is equal, not only in his rights and privileges, but in his responsibilities to the government.*

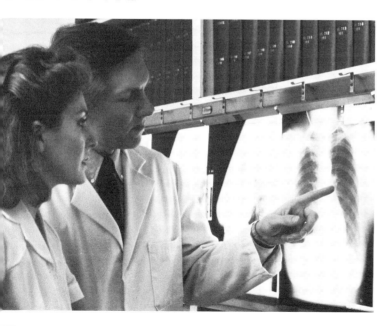

Photographs by Harold M. Lambert

29

ference once a candidate is in office that promises were made that the candidate does not intend to keep. But even this is a reflection on the people themselves, as if they can be taken in by clever rhetoric or impressed with promises they know cannot possibly be fulfilled. There is no way such a statement can be made without revealing in some way, somehow, people inadequacy in terms of people sovereignty.

The fact is that those who come to the United States Senate have to do something in order to get the people to elect them. They have to present themselves to the people in one way or another. The people have the responsibility of evaluating what they hear and see and read about a possible candidate in order to vote intelligently and put into office that candidate who will most responsibly represent his or her constituency.

Our political system is a representative system. The people vote for those candidates they believe will most completely represent them in the elected office for which they are running. The candidates must present themselves and convince the people of their credibility, their integrity, their qualifications. The candidate must persuade the people that his platform, his program, his agenda, if elected, will most nearly conform to the agenda, the interests and the concerns of the people who go to the polls.

In a series of tributes to retiring senators on the last day of the 99th Congress, Senator Spark Matsunaga told of an experience he had as a law student. His senator from Hawaii asked him, as a World War II veteran, to come to Washington to lobby for Hawaiian statehood. He came to see Senator Russell Long of Louisiana and was received without an appointment. After listening to his appeal, Senator Long said to him, "Young man, you must remember that a U.S. senator is primarily interested in two things: one, to be elected, and two, to be re-elected. So, don't come to me; go to my constituents. If my constituents tell me that I should support Hawaiian statehood, I will."

Senator Matsunaga also told the following regarding retiring Senator Tom Eagleton of Missouri: "As I have observed earlier,

Mr. President, he is a workhorse, strong as a Missouri mule in his convictions that the welfare of the people must always reign supreme in all legislative endeavors."[3]

In the case of the United States Senate, which has 100 members, each member represents all the people in his home state as well as millions of others in the region of the United States from which the senator comes. He is sent to the Senate with the understanding that his office will responsibly represent local, state and regional concerns, and national interests when it comes to international affairs. This means the average senator is inundated with an almost unlimited number of interests and issues, most of which are conflicting, and all competing for the attention, interest, and decision of 100 senators.

This is the reality that is the American political system. By its very nature it is cumbersome, slow, inefficient, but it is the only system presently, and for the past 200 years, that guarantees the greatest good for the largest number. It provides, as no other system, the maximum protection of minorities, the possibility of justice to all the people. It is a process that, because of its slowness and inefficiency, can provoke the most criticism by those who place the greatest demands on it. But, thank God, it is a system that not only allows dissent, but encourages, promotes and protects it.

Remembering how difficult it was for our little neighborhood organization to resolve a zoning problem, I have great appreciation for the deliberation, debate and decision process of the United States Congress. Impatience—at times, alienation—the many extended meetings—cause one to wonder how anything can ever be decided in the United States Senate with its relentless pressures of competing, conflicting, controversial issues that will not go away until they are somehow handled.

Think of these diverse concerns, agendas and issues that are America, realizing that this list only scratches the surface: timber in the Pacific Northwest, water in the deserts of the Southwest, cotton and fruit in California and Florida, wheat and corn in the

Photographs by Harold M. Lambert

*k of these diverse concerns,
*das and issues that are
*rica, realizing that this list
scratches the surface:
*er in the Pacific Northwest,
*r in the deserts of the
*hwest, cotton and fruit in
*fornia and Florida, wheat
corn in the Plains states,
*n the south and central states,
*cco and cotton in the
*heast, fisheries and textiles
*e Northeast, beef cattle in
*s, dairy products in
*onsin. The diversity goes on
on and each of these, plus
*dreds more, compete for the
lative attention of our
*esentatives in Washington,

*.

Plains states, oil in the south and central states, tobacco and cotton in the Southeast, fisheries and textiles in the Northeast, beef cattle in Texas, dairy products in Wisconsin. The diversity goes on and on and each of these, plus hundreds more, compete for the legislative attention of our representatives in Washington, D.C.

"The squeaky wheel gets the grease" is a truism that has constant relevance in a representative government. If the people do not understand these realities of a representative government, if they expect instant action on their interests, disappointment is inevitable. If they allow disappointment to cause them to withdraw from involvement and abdicate their people sovereignty, they are surrendering their rights and responsibilities to special interests that understand the process and do everything in their power to make it work for their own benefit.

Incidentally, one of the most important aspects in understanding the United States Senate is that much, even most, of the work is done in committee. Bills presented on the floor of the Senate are referred to committee, where committee either votes to send the bill back to the floor for debate and vote or declines to do so.

Often during the years I have been chaplain of the Senate, I have been amazed at the confusion or the wonder of visitors in the gallery of the Senate when there are no senators on the floor, or perhaps very few. Not uncommonly, a senator will make a speech on the floor when it is virtually empty for the purpose of getting it into the record. When a speech is made, members of the senator's staff who deal with that particular legislation will be paying careful attention to the speech in order that the senator can examine it in the light of future debating if it has to do with legislation and voting.

The fact that the senators are not on the floor does not mean they are not working. As a matter of fact, every senator is a member of several committees or subcommittees, so long before a bill gets to the floor he is involved in exceedingly active legislative work.

These special interests, most commonly (though not exclusively) in the form of political action committees and lobbyists, exert tremendous pressure on legislation. The political action committees (or PACs, as they are commonly called) provide the lion's share of campaign funds for candidates to legislative office. They naturally expect, and have a right to expect, a return on their investment. In one way or another, they will constantly remind the candidate of whose campaign they supported financially.

If individual citizens, for whatever reason, fail to support their candidate with campaign funds, if they are willing to allow PACs to do most, if not all, the financing, they shouldn't be surprised when their interests are subordinated to the interests of political action committees or lobbyists. To put it simply, representative government is a pressure game at its best, or in the words with which we began this section "The squeaky wheel gets the grease."

If private citizens allow these realities to make them indifferent or cynical, thus abandoning the political process so their voice is unheard, they surrender to the special interests by their abdication from people sovereignty.

The remarkable political system given to us by our founding fathers was designed to keep public servants accountable to the people by whose consent they receive their just powers. When the people refuse to exercise their sovereignty, the accountability of public servants switches from the people to special interests.

The secret ballot and the private voting booth is the very heart of our political system, the first point of attack, directly or indirectly, by those who would abuse the system. People power is exercised preeminently at the polls. In terms of our governmental system the most tragic facts of the past three decades in America has been the decreasing number of citizens registering to vote and the alarming decrease of registered voters who go to the polls.

In 1960 when Senator John F. Kennedy was elected to the presidency of the United States the number of eligible voters who went to the polls was 62.8 percent. In the presidential election of

*People power is exercised preeminently at the polls. In terms of our governmental system the most tragic facts of the past three decades in America has been the decreasing number of citizens registering to vote and the alarming decrease of registered voters who go to the polls.*

1984 only 53.9 percent of those eligible to vote went to the polls. That means that almost 50 percent of the people who were eligible to vote did not do so in that election. The explanations or excuses for not voting are not only invalid, they reveal a tragic ignorance of the fundamental basis for our political system—the sovereignty of the people.

"My one vote will not make any difference" is often given to justify absence from the polls. The number is legion of those situations where one vote made a difference. Not to vote is actually to vote—possibly for a candidate you would not want to represent you. Be very sure that there are forces organized and dedicated to getting people to the polls who will promote their special interests. You may neglect to vote, but remember, there are those who will be at the polls whose vote is not in your interests—quite possibly in direct opposition to your interests. The private voting booth and the secret ballot are the cornerstone of our political system; if they are neglected, the system breaks down.

Voting requires intelligent preparation. It means knowing the candidates and knowing the issues. It means knowing the voting record of incumbents. It means certifying the credibility and integrity of the candidate. Integrity is vital; it is essential. Voting records are instructive, but they are not necessarily the final criterion, especially when consideration is limited to a single issue. The integrity of the candidate is of primary concern. Is he or she qualified, trustworthy, experienced, intelligent?

The importance of this preparation by the voter cannot be exaggerated in these days when television plays such a large part in political campaigns. Television actually deals very little with the issues. Its value is in name recognition, candidate image and public relations.

Here is a true story of a young man running for a state legislature in 1986. He had been defeated in the previous attempt but had learned a great deal in the process. In his first attempt he took issues seriously, but he learned tragically that the issues made very little difference. In his second effort to be elected as a state legislator he is attempting to raise a million dollars for his campaign, much of which will be used for television. His appeals for funds are made mostly to political action committees and he says his only real contact with his constituency is television. In other words, it seems that he expects to get very little money for his political campaign from the people; with less effort and energy he can appeal to the political action committees with greater success.

Two items in two different issues of *U.S. News and World Report* give insight into the superficiality of political campaigns that depend primarily upon television. On a page called "Washington Whispers," August 25, 1986, the very last paragraph reads as follows: "Brace yourself for a flood of 'feel good' political commercials. Campaign consultants report that surveys show voters are responding only to TV ads long on upbeat messages, short on substance or negative attacks."[4] TV campaigns tend to lower the quality of any political campaign and, incidentally, prove nothing about issues.

In the September 8, 1986, issue of *U.S. News and World Report* on page 19, entitled "Politics," in a boxed article with the title "Downhome Commercials," we have these comments: "Welcome to the feel-good brand of political television commercials in campaign '86.

"Media consultants agree that issues will rank second to style in TV political messages this fall. Warmth and compassion, backed up by folksy scenery and spritely music, are in. Aim: give voters a comfortable impression of a candidate they aren't likely to meet or hear in person."[5]

Later on the same page we find this quotation: "Media costs, which eat up 50 percent or more of many campaign budgets, are skyrocketing. A 30-second prime time ad on a highly rated TV program in the New York market can run as high as $22,000. A similar ad in North Dakota will cost only $300.

"A big chunk of the money goes to the media consultants. Most sign with campaigns for up to $75,000 for their creative work, but they usually get an additional 15 percent in commissions from media buys. That means a consultant in a statewide campaign in multi-market states like New York or California might knock down some $750,000 for a single candidate."[6]

But the exercise of people's sovereignty consists of much more than watching TV or spending a few minutes in the privacy of a voting booth on election day. One must give consideration to other matters that will guide him in his vote. This requires knowing something about the candidates, having some understanding of the issues and responsibilities of the office to which the candidate aspires. This means serious reading, listening and thinking, as well as discussion with others. It means ascertaining the integrity of the candidate, which, incidentally, is not necessarily discovered by studying a voting record, especially on a single issue basis.

When the election is over and the victors have been installed in office, the exercise of people sovereignty does not end. The responsible citizen must do his best to stay informed about the issues as they develop, to know his representatives at the various levels of government, and to maintain contact with them as much as possible. This is the only way these representatives have of knowing what the citizen thinks and what his views are concerning the various issues to be legislated.

One of the surprises that I have encountered during my time in Washington, especially since being chaplain of the Senate, is that many people do not even know who their representatives are. They cannot name their senators nor their representatives in the House, nor the chief justice of the United States, and sometimes not even their governor or the state legislator who represents them. This indicates an almost total indifference to those in authority and a failure to understand the fundamental principle of our democratic republic that the people are sovereign, not the government.

The truth is our representatives want to know what the people think. They have staff members whose job it is to discover this. They appreciate correspondence. They take it seriously. It ought to be said in this context that a form letter, which obviously was dictated by some organization and sent out by the tens of thousands, has less of an impact upon a representative than a personal letter clearly written by the citizen himself. Although mass mailings are not ignored and are probably always counted, the personal letter from an individual citizen has significant impact in the life and business of the legislator.

It is common on the floor of the Senate to hear senators tell how many letters they have received on each side of a certain issue. This is a familiar part of debate. And it is significant how the atmosphere of the Senate can change when the senators return after a recess during which they have heard from the people.

Important also to this process is the personal contacts that citizens make when they are in Washington, the state capital or the vicinity of the city hall. An effort ought to be made, occasionally at least, to have a personal visit, however brief, with one's representative. This is not often possible because representatives are normally very busy and there are almost impossible demands upon their time and energy. But even if the representative is unable to see the constituent, the fact that the citizen has made the attempt at contact makes a difference, and it registers with the representative. Contacts with a member of the senator's staff will be made known to the senator.

Furthermore, those who work in the federal government make regular visits to their home states. They have local offices and they speak at many meetings in an effort to maintain contact with their constituents. Learning when one's representative will be in his home office and making a brief personal contact with him is a very important way to maintain a relationship fundamental to the exercise of people sovereignty.

Stop and think. What makes a TV program, a magazine or a newspaper successful? It's the number who view and read. In the final analysis people power is the real power in a democracy. People determine the success—or failure—of the centers of influence in our culture.

Democracy is a slow and inefficient process, but it is the best form of government yet to be tried in history. Totalitarianism is much more efficient and it moves much faster, but that is because leadership is not in office by the will of the people nor does it have to be concerned about the will of the people. From our founding fathers we inherited a system that, though it has many weaknesses, is designed to provide the best for the most, while at the same time protecting the rights of minorities—even a minority of one. As a matter of fact, much of the time of some senators' staff members is spent on precisely this issue—the need of a minority of one. Thousands of individual personal problems come to the office of the senator or the representative, and they cannot be ignored. They must be dealt with. One senator said he responded to an average of 1,500 constituent requests monthly.

The legislative process in a democracy is slow because every side, every implication of an issue must be examined, and it must be examined in the light of the whole: every state, every city, every region, every special interest. It involves compromise, which, incidentally, does not necessarily mean compromise of principle. Senators from the East have to make trades with senators from the West to get the best for their people, and vice versa. So it is with senators of the North and the South, Northwest and the Southeast, the Northeast and the Southwest, etc. Just the issue of agriculture, for example, is not a simple matter. It involves many different groups—beef cattle versus dairy cattle, tobacco versus wheat, coffee versus barley, etc.

My wife and I are members of a small neighborhood organization in Arlington, Virginia. Within the bounds of our neighborhood is an undeveloped 20-acre tract. It is zoned for private dwellings. A developer has contracted for the purchase of that 20 acres on the condition that he may build a senior citizens' residence there.

Our little neighborhood group has had five meetings concerning this matter over a lengthy period of time. The meetings are often emotional and sometimes quite hostile. The community has been before the zoning board and the county council, who themselves have to struggle, not only with the desires of the neighborhood, but with the needs of the larger community as well. The process is inefficient and it is slow, but it is the best way devised by man.

People movements are integral to the democratic process and people movements not uncommonly are expressed through activism in one form or another, by few or by many. Activism is one way of getting the attention of those in authority and, incidentally, the press. Often activism is the only way to get the attention of authority and the press. Hopefully, however, activism will never become violent. Certainly, the one committed to the Prince of Peace and obedient to His commands would eschew violence.

But the fact is that our American democratic system began with a violent revolution. As one reads the history of the precolonial and colonial days, one is impressed with the patience and restraint of the colonists with regard to the king. Every possible effort at peaceful solutions was tried with little effectiveness generally. The colonies did not want armed rebellion and did not

*"Pulling down the statue of George III by the Sons of Freedom at the bowling green, City of New York, 1776." The pulling down of the statue was a gesture symbolizing the crumbling of an old political order and the emergence of a new one. In its infancy the (American) rebellion was defensive and nonviolent, becoming armed rebellion only as the throne ignored or repelled every effort at negotiation.*

seek it, but it was forced upon them by the intransigence of the British throne.

In its infancy rebellion was primarily defensive and became armed rebellion only as the throne ignored or repelled every effort at negotiation. The remarkable thing about the American revolution is that our founding fathers gave us precisely what they said they were fighting for. They gave us a representative form of government, a government of the people, by the people, for the people, which is still working today after 200 years.

One of the most impressive things to me since I have been in the Senate is the seriousness with which public servants take the Constitution. They never forget that, when sworn into office, they solemnly promise to protect the Constitution.

Activism is not inconsistent on the part of the children of the Kingdom living in an alien world, much of which is in opposition to the King of kings and the Lord of lords. On the occasion of Simon Peter's recognition of and witness to Jesus Christ as the Messiah at Caesarea, Philippi, Jesus commended Peter: "Blessed are you, Simon son of Jonah, for this was not revealed to you by man, but by my Father in heaven. And I tell you that you are Peter, and on this rock I will build my church, and the gates of Hades will not overcome it" (Matthew 16:17,18).

The gates of Hades (hell) are not offensive; (they) are defensive. They do not go out to war—they protect the fortress. They are not active—they are passive, designed to resist assault. By implication, there are times when the Church of Jesus Christ must take the offensive against the gates of hell. The Church must attack in the remarkable promise and prospect that she is invincible and indestructible. Activism under certain circumstances is proper and sometimes necessary for the person who takes Christ and His Kingdom seriously.

In a letter to Abigail Adams, written from Paris, dated February 22, 1787, Thomas Jefferson recognized the necessity of people resistance to government when he wrote, "The spirit of resistance to government is so valuable on certain occasions, that I wish

The text inscribed on the wall reads:

...D THESE TRUTHS TO BE SELF-
...THAT ALL MEN ARE CREATED
...T THEY ARE ENDOWED BY THEIR
...WITH CERTAIN INALIENABLE
...AMONG THESE ARE LIFE, LIBERTY
...E PURSUIT OF HAPPINESS, THAT
...RE THESE RIGHTS GOVERNMENTS
...STITUTED AMONG MEN, WE—
...NLY PUBLISH AND DECLARE, THAT
...COLONIES ARE AND OF RIGHT
...T TO BE FREE AND INDEPENDENT
...—AND FOR THE SUPPORT OF THIS
...RATION, WITH A FIRM RELIANCE
...E PROTECTION OF DIVINE
...DENCE WE MUTUALLY PLEDGE
...OUR FORTUNES AND OUR
...HONOR

*"Statue of Thomas Jefferson."* Thomas Jefferson recognized the necessity of people resistance to government when he wrote, *"The spirit of resistance to government is so valuable on certain occasions, that I wish it to be always kept alive. It will often be exercised when wrong, but better so than not to be exercised at all. I like a little rebellion now and then."*

Photograph by Harold M. Lambert

it to be always kept alive. It will often be exercised when wrong, but better so than not to be exercised at all. I like a little rebellion now and then."[7]

Anthony Campollo, popular leader, lecturer and speaker, sociologist and evangelist, said it most succinctly in his book, *Partly Right*:

"It is the allegiance to a belief that the Kingdom of God is something that can and must be approached within human society. From the time of the pilgrims, Americans have been imbued with the sense of being on a divine mission. They have believed that it is their calling to establish a society which more closely approximates the will of God than any since the best days of ancient Israel. Americans have sought to hold their institutions to the same ideal for justice that the Hebrew prophets would have commanded, and they have endeavored to establish in their communities a fellowship that imitates the fellowship of the early church.

"The American people have not deluded themselves into thinking they could realize a Utopian dream . . . . Nevertheless, they have preached that it is the duty of all Americans to work together constantly to improve their institutions so that more and more their society might be likened to the Kingdom which Christ will establish at eschaton.

"Government in America never has been viewed as simply a necessary evil. Instead, middle class Americans have viewed it as an instrument through which society could be increasingly perfected. They have viewed government with ambivalence. On the one hand, they have ridiculed its bureaucratic failures and feared its encroachments on personal liberties. On the other hand, they have looked to it with hope, believing that in spite of all its shortcomings, it is still an instrument through which God's people can work constantly to make America more like that which their God planned for it to be."[8]

"We hold these Truths to be self-evident, that all Men are created equal, that they are endowed by their Creator with certain unalienable Rights . . . to secure these Rights, Governments are instituted among Men, deriving their just Powers from the Consent of the Governed."

(Declaration of Independence)

---

God of Creation, we thank you for our political system, its uniqueness in history, and the prosperous, powerful republic which is its product. We thank you for the fundamental principle that sovereignty belongs to the people and that government receives its powers from them. Help us to realize, Lord, that if the people fail to understand this—if they ignore or neglect their sovereignty—the system inevitably will break down. Awaken us to the peril of the republic if people abdicate their sovereignty and quicken the people to their indispensable responsibility. We pray in His name who is the source of all power, Amen.

Prayer in The Senate—March 14, 1986

CHAPTER 3

# The Relevance of Prayer

---

**W**hen the Senate was debating confirmation of the president's appointment of Associate Justice Sandra O'Connor to the Supreme Court, I spent the entire day on the floor of the Senate listening to the debate. Six hours had been allowed for the debate although it was a foregone conclusion that she was going to be confirmed. Six hours proved unnecessary.

Many senators did not speak and those who did began with the assurance that they were going to vote to confirm Mrs. O'Connor as a justice to the Supreme Court. Occasionally a senator would include a caveat indicating his expectations of the justice's position on specific issues.

There was a wonderful spirit of unity in the Senate that day. The galleries were filled, and when the time came for the vote the atmosphere was electric. Even though there was no opposition,

*From the time of our forefathers, prayer has been a powerful and effective force in the shaping and influencing of our nation. George Washington realized this, even as he knelt in prayer at Valley Forge.*

no sense of the vote going any other way than for confirmation, it was the spirit in the Senate that was exciting and expectant. The vote was 99-0 in favor of Mrs. O'Connor's confirmation, one senator being involuntarily absent that day.

Listening to the debate on the floor of the Senate, I asked myself if I had ever prayed privately for the Supreme Court. Without fail we prayed for the Supreme Court regularly in the Sunday morning pastoral prayer at Fourth Presbyterian Church, just as we did for local and national leaders. But I couldn't remember ever praying for the Supreme Court in my own private devotions or worship.

That evening (I believe in divine providence) the Christian Legal Society had a dinner on Capitol Hill, and they had asked me to conclude the dinner with a few brief remarks. There were perhaps 125 people present. The burden of the program was a report by three brilliant and articulate young attorneys concerning the issues that impinged upon faith, the church and religion in general, which were scheduled before the U.S. Supreme Court during that session. The young men presented the issues very clearly, and one could feel the concern and apprehension aroused by their report.

Finally, I was introduced for the closing remarks. I reported to the people my experience on the floor of the Senate earlier that day concerning the appointment of Mrs. O'Connor. In conclusion, I told them I was going to ask them a question that did not require an audible response, but simply an answer in their own hearts.

Then I asked, "How many of you pray for the Supreme Court in your private worship?" It wasn't necessary to have an audible answer. One could sense the silent, collective answer. When we were dismissed, many of the people at that dinner expressed appreciation for the remarks and the question. I believe, with one or two exceptions, they all acknowledged that they never thought to pray for the Supreme Court. They had often criticized it, had been anxious and angry sometimes about its decisions, but it had never occurred to them to pray for the Supreme Court.

I've told this little story in many different places all over the country, always with the same reaction. It is very common to criticize the Supreme Court, to be angry with its judgments, but never to pray for it.

What truly concerns me is when I visit various churches and find that several of them fail to include intercession for local or national government in their pastoral prayers. Rarely is there a prayer for the president and his family or the vice president and his family, for members of Congress, for the Supreme Court, for the governor, the state legislator, the mayor, the city council, the police officers, etc. I have been absolutely amazed and profoundly concerned at how few churches include in their Sunday morning prayers intercession for public servants.

This is not just an unfortunate oversight on the part of the people of God. It is in direct disobedience to the Word of God. Prayer for men and women in public life is not optional for those who take their faith seriously. Prayer is mandatory—prayerlessness is inexcusable.

The Apostle Paul, in writing to his son in the faith, the young pastor, Timothy, following introductory comments in the first chapter of his first epistle to Timothy, begins with his instruction as follows:

*I urge, then, first of all, that requests, prayers, intercession and thanksgiving be made for everyone—for kings and all those in authority, that we may live peaceful and quiet lives in all godliness and holiness. This is good, and pleases God our Savior, who wants all men to be saved and to come to a knowledge of the truth. For there is one God and one mediator between God and men, the man Christ Jesus* (1 Timothy 2:1-5).

Here the Apostle Paul is instructing a young pastor as to his responsibilities in the church. He begins his instructions by saying "first of all" and then exhorts that prayer, requests and intercession be made for all people, for kings and for those who are in authority. To paraphrase what Paul says, "As a matter of first importance, pray for all people and for rulers and public servants."

If we believe that the Scriptures are inspired by God, then the Apostle Paul was writing to Timothy, led by the Holy Spirit. In other words, the Spirit of God was instructing this young pastor that prayer was a matter of first importance; included in that exhortation is prayer for leadership, for rulers, for those who have authority.

If that had been all the Apostle Paul had written to the young pastor, it should be enough to make all who follow Christ realize that, if we take the Scriptures seriously, we are under the mandate to pray for those who govern. However, Paul continues with some very strong arguments as to the consequences of such prayer: "that we may live peaceful and quiet lives in all godliness and holiness."

Think about that! Faithfulness in intercession for leadership promises a desirable social order—a quiet, peaceable life, godly and holy. What a contrast to the social decay around us today—turbulence, violence, sin, irreverence, terrorism, and the relentless threat of war. The Apostle Paul, writing under the inspiration of the Holy Spirit, connects a constructive social environment with faithful intercession for all people, especially those in authority, those who govern.

But he does not leave it there. After declaring this to be good and acceptable in the sight of God, our Saviour, he adds "Who wants all men to be saved and to come to a knowledge of the truth." Paul connects faithfulness in intercession to effectiveness in evangelism and mission. There are many places in the world today where missionaries or evangelists are not welcome. They would not be granted a visa if they declared their purpose in going to be that of serving as a missionary, evangelist or a preacher.

Even in the United States, during the past two decades, the Supreme Court has ruled in ways that impinge upon our freedom of worship. More and more secularization is driving faith out of public life into the private sector. One cannot help but wonder how different decisions by the Supreme Court might have been if those who are most critical of those decisions had been the most faithful in interceding for the Supreme Court.

If there were no other motivation or incentive, exhortation or instruction in the Bible than the mandate to pray for those who rule over us, Paul's word to Timothy would be sufficient to induce us, indeed, compel us to pray. We are not listening to the Spirit of God. We are not taking seriously the Scriptures. We are not acting out what we profess to believe about the Bible as our final authority, ultimate authority, absolute authority, if we do not take seriously this essential matter of prayer.

But there is an even more urgent reason to pray. In the most basic sense prayer is the ultimate resistance to evil. The Apostle Paul expresses it clearly in an earnest exhortation and instruction:

*Finally, be strong in the Lord and in his mighty power. Put on the full armor of God so that you can take your stand against the devil's schemes. For our struggle is not against flesh and blood, but against the rulers, against the authorities, against the powers of this dark world and against the spiritual forces of evil in the heavenly realms. Therefore put on the full armor of God, so that when the day of evil comes, you may be able to stand your ground, and after you have done everything, to stand. Stand firm then, with the belt of truth buckled around your waist, with the breastplate of righteousness in place, and with your feet fitted with the readiness that comes from the gospel of peace. In addition to all this, take up the shield of faith, with which you can extinguish all the flaming arrows of the evil one. Take the helmet of salvation and the sword of the Spirit, which is the word of God* (Ephesians 6:10-17).

Having defined the real conflict as spiritual rather than material, and having identified the real enemy, Paul exhorts us to "put on the full armor of God," which is the only adequate defense against the enemy.

Then he defines the warfare.

*And pray in the Spirit on all occasions with all kinds of prayers and requests. With this in mind, be alert and always keep on praying for all the saints* (Ephesians 6:18).

The real conflict is spiritual. The real enemy is invisible. His masterpiece is his incognito. His most subtle strategy is to convince us of his nonexistence.

It is not uncommon in these days to hear about Satan worshipers. They should be taken seriously and not ignored. But of far greater concern are those who do not believe in a personal devil—who deny his existence and are therefore free to ignore this threat. Obviously no one is afraid of something he doesn't believe exists. The real enemy is then free to make his assault upon the unwary, masquerading as a being with horns and a tail and red skin. He works his wily subterfuge in an environment where he is simply not taken seriously. He is a joke. He is a myth.

In the first three chapters of the Bible we are introduced to the supreme conflict, which transcends all other conflicts and from which all other conflicts derive. The first four words in Genesis present to us the Author of all reality, the Author of life and truth and righteousness and justice: "In the beginning God . . . " The first three words of Genesis 3 present the author of evil, the consummate deceiver, the father of lies: "Now the serpent . . . " He is described as "more crafty than any of the wild animals the Lord God had made."

The Bible nowhere attempts to prove the reality of God or the reality of the devil; the Bible simply declares these two realities. God is the creator, the devil is a creature. From this point on the Bible records the cosmic conflict between God and the devil, truth and error, light and darkness.

One subtle strategy of the evil one is to keep us thinking about evils in the plural rather than the evil one who is the author of evils. If he can keep us fighting evils rather than the evil one himself, he continues to win his victory. He is quite willing for us to win some battles, but he is determined to win the war.

As citizens of the Kingdom of God we are compelled to resist evil in whatever way it manifests itself. We cannot condone divorce, child abuse, abortion, drug or alcohol dependence, etc. We must do all in our power to deal with them, but they are symptoms of the primal evil, and we must never allow ourselves to forget that. Otherwise we will win some battles, but we will lose the war.

In Ephesians 6, the apostle indicates that evil is not simply personal, individualistic or social; evil is institutional, bureaucratic, structural. The basic struggle is "against the rulers, against the authorities, against the powers of this dark world and against the spiritual forces of evil in the heavenly realms" (Ephesians 6:12).

In the summer of 1986 Reverend Doctor Allan Bosack, courageous and dedicated leader of South Africa, was speaking at a local black church in Washington, D.C. Though he was urged to speak on the theme of sanctions he declined. When he was introduced to speak to the congregation he stood in the pulpit a long time, staring silently at the people. When he finally began to speak, he said, "You Americans are far too sophisticated to understand the personal, palpable presence of the satanic."[9] How spiritually insightful, provocative and penetrating!

In this, as in other matters, the Bible gives us the clearest understanding of evil in history. If we disregard the Bible and its truth and attempt to oppose evil in our human wisdom and strength only, seeing evil as a natural, rather than a supernatural phenomenon, we are doomed to futility.

As a matter of fact, history seems to confirm this over and over. Despite all the laws that are passed, all the effort spent, all the organizations developed, all the money and energy expended to fight social evil, the evils not only aren't solved, they increase epidemically. This has certainly been true in the last two decades of our national life.

We cannot ignore the various evils which confront and destroy; we must recognize the fundamental fact that there is a solidarity, a unity, a oneness of evil. As important as it is to identify and resist every variety of evil, it is absolutely essential that we remember

that all the evils have a common root. We must be concerned about all the evils, but history and experience indicate that tackling any one of these evils or combination of them while we ignore the author of evil is a futile effort.

The Ten Commandments prescribed the perfect law of God, but God's perfect moral law does not eliminate evil, it only identifies it, as an X-ray identifies disease. If the perfect moral law of God cannot produce a perfect social order, certainly those statutes legislated by human beings cannot do so. Think of the thousands of laws that have been and are being passed by the various legislative bodies of the world; in spite of them all, the evils not only continue, they increase.

This is at the heart of the nonfulfillment that Paul speaks of in his letter to the Romans: "The creation waits in eager expectation for the sons of God to be revealed. For the creation was subjected to frustration, not by its own choice, but by the will of the one who subjected it" (Romans 8:19,20). This does not mean that legislation should not take place. Law is essential in human history as a deterrent, or restraint, against evil. As Paul declares in 1 Timothy, chapter one, "Law is . . . for lawbreakers" (v. 9).

"We know that the law is good if a man uses it properly. We also know that law is made not for good men but for lawbreakers and rebels, the ungodly and sinful" (1 Timothy 1:8-9).

It is impossible for the follower of Christ who takes his faith seriously to ignore the various evils. He finds them intolerable and he will in every way he can resist them and fight to eliminate them. This is instinctive in the heart and mind of the people of the Kingdom of God, but they are deluded if they believe they can destroy or eliminate these evils while at the same time failing to take seriously the source of evil.

To do so is like being preoccupied with putting out secondary fires started by the scattering of ashes while ignoring the central fire from which the peripheral fires spring. Or to put it another way, it is like being preoccupied with the symptoms of a disease while ignoring the disease itself. Symptoms are effects and must

*In the tortured eyes and emaciated bodies of the survivors of such death camps as Auschwitz and Dachau, we see the evidence of evil. We cannot ignore the various evils that confront and destroy . . . but history and experience indicate that tackling any one of these evils or combination of them while we ignore the author of evil is a futile attempt.*

be taken seriously in order to discover the cause of the symptoms and then deal with it.

The Apostle Paul describes prayer as fundamental in this warfare. He says, "Pray in the Spirit on all occasions with all kinds of prayers and requests" (Ephesians 6:18). Prayer therefore is an essential and indispensable element in the struggle against evil.

For what then do we pray? Paul urges "that requests, prayers, intercession and thanksgiving be made for everyone—for kings and all those in authority" (1 Timothy 2:1,2). It goes without saying that a child of the Kingdom should be a faithful citizen in the world. The essential, unarguable, indispensable expression of this citizenship is prayer.

Though our prayers should be for all, there is an irreducible minimum for every child of God. We all have one president, one vice president, one Supreme Court, two senators, and one representative; one governor, one legislator, one county representative, one mayor, and one representative on the city council. Each of us has a police force and fire department with their chiefs. These are all appointed by God to have authority over us. To fail to pray for this irreducible minimum is to fail in good citizenship.

Intercession, of course, should not stop there. There are many more federal, state and local authorities. There are school boards, school superintendents, school principals and teachers. We have not fulfilled our responsibility as good citizens if we fail or refuse to pray for all of these public servants. No matter what else we do, if we do not pray, we lose the battles—we lose the war.

# CHAPTER 4

# Christians in Government

One legitimate and practical form of activism is to seek public office. As a matter of fact, this is probably the most effective method. Throughout the history of the Church, its greatest influence has not been its institutions, its eloquent preachers and evangelists, its powerful administrators and leaders, its programs and its projects, not even its radio and television ministries. The maximum influence of the Church in history has been the aggregate of individual believers where they are in their homes and neighborhoods and jobs and social circles, day in, day out, week after week, in the normal routines of life.

It is not the influence of the Church when the people are gathered in the sanctuary on Sunday, but when the sanctuary is empty and the people are scattered between Sundays, penetrating their homes, their neighborhoods, their social circles, their schools, their jobs—penetrating, pervading, permeating their whole environment and the organizations and institutions around them. It is the influence of a righteous presence in the midst of an unbelieving world. What is said is important, what is done is important, but fundamental to both proclamation and performance, both word and deed, is a righteous presence.

One interesting and frustrating aspect of the church/state debate has been the confusion of a comment by Thomas Jefferson made to the Baptists of Danbury, Connecticut in 1802. The paragraph in which he made this statement is as follows:

"Believing that religion is a matter which lies solely between man and his God, that he owes account to none other for his faith or his worship, that the legislative powers of government reach actions only, and not opinions, I contemplate with sovereign reverence that act of the whole American people which declared that their legislature should make no law respecting an establishment of religion, or prohibiting the free exercise thereof, thus building a wall of separation between Church and State."[10]

The confusion to which I am referring is the last statement in that paragraph, "thus building a wall of separation between Church and State." It seems clear in the context of that paragraph and in all of the other things that Jefferson said and wrote during his public life that the point that he was making was, in effect, that government should stay out of religion, that legislatures should make no laws that interfere with religious practice or worship or belief.

However, the interpretation, at least in the last few decades, that has been given to that statement is that not only must government stay out of the Church, but the Church must stay out of government. It is incorrect to interpret this statement of Thomas Jefferson's in that way, inasmuch as his own religious beliefs had a great deal of influence in his writing of the Declaration of Independence and in all of his involvement in public policy during his public life.

Nevertheless, when one refers to the first amendment today, immediately Thomas Jefferson's statement comes to mind and is

*The Declaration of Independence is considered the single most important document of American history. Written by Thomas Jefferson with the help of John Adams and Benjamin Franklin, it was intended to explain and justify to the American colonies, England, and the rest of the world the colonial decision for separation from Britain. For the men of the Revolution it laid down the principles for which they fought. "We hold these truths to be self-evident, that all men are created equal, that they are endowed by their Creator with certain unalienable Rights, that among these are Life, Liberty and the pursuit of Happiness."*

Photo from the archives of the Library of Congress

often, if not always, equated with the first amendment. On the basis of this interpretation we are being told over and over again that the Church has no business being involved in government or in the political process or in the influencing of public policy, which to me seems as far removed from what was in the minds of our founding fathers, including Thomas Jefferson, as is possible.

"Congress shall make no law respecting an establishment of religion, or prohibiting the free exercise thereof . . . " Those two clauses compose what the first amendment has to say about religion and government. If words mean anything, what our founding fathers were intending was that government under no circumstances should give preferential treatment to any particular religious group, and, secondly, that government should in no way interfere in any person's or group's free exercise of faith, religious practice or worship.

Not a word of those two clauses in the first amendment separates the Church from the state. It can be inferred, I believe, from the first amendment that, should any individual religious person or group of persons be given, by election or appointment, a place of authority in government, the law prohibits them from imposing their religious beliefs, practices or worship upon others.

There was precedent, of course, for this in the state churches of Europe. Indeed, for this reason, among others, our founding fathers came to the shores of America. Though certain religious leaders in some colonies initially misused legal power, this nation's founders did not intend to create a situation where the coalition of religion and government would result in the kind of oppression from which they were fleeing. In other words, no person or group of persons who might, by whatever means, obtain a position of power in government would have the right to impose their beliefs, practices or worship upon those of other religious persuasions or upon those of no religious persuasion whatsoever.

In this respect it is obvious that there is a wall separating church and state, but it certainly does not mean that people of any religious persuasion are forbidden to be involved in government or in influencing public policy through acceptable methods and means.

On February 18, 1986, former President Jimmy Carter addressed faculty and student body of Messiah College, Grantham, Pennsylvania, on the theme of religion and American foreign policy. In his address the president witnessed to his own faith from childhood, his practice of it, his worship, and his convictions, which, of course, he brought with him into the White House.

He did not abandon his faith when he became the president of the United States. He was the same person with the same convictions. He continued attending church as regularly as possible and indeed continued to teach Sunday School class in his church in Washington. But President Carter made it very clear in his address that, as president of the United States, he was president of all the people—those who shared his beliefs, those who believed differently than he, and those who had no religious beliefs at all. He made it clear that the responsibilities of high office in the United States limit anyone in elected or appointed office from imposing his faith upon others.

In the appendices of this book we have printed portions of this address of President Carter in the hopes that it will provide some clarification for those who suffer the illusion—and it is an illusion—that the United States began as a Christian nation, from which it has now departed, and that Christians should do everything in their power to restore that status to our land despite the greatly increased pluralism that exists in our country today.

In the past 40 years, circumstances have brought to the United States those of many religious persuasions. They include Muslims, Buddhists, Hindus, and many of no religious persuasion at all. This is not to mention the large Jewish population in the United States who have been American citizens from the very beginning and who have made an incalculable contribution to everything that is good about our nation and its political processes.

I am not saying that Christians do not have the right, indeed the responsibility, consistent with their evangelical convictions, to evangelize and love those of other persuasions or no persuasions, just as Christian missionaries cover the earth in every land for this very purpose. I am saying that Christians, however zealous, do not have the right to seek power or authority in government or any other organization apart from the Church itself in order to impose their religious beliefs, practices or worship upon others.

At the risk of being misunderstood, it seems to me that a comment is relevant at this point, which is actually more in the nature of a footnote than a part of the argument. There is a way of thinking among contemporary evangelicals, based apparently upon certain eschatalogical convictions, that tends to equate the United States of America with the nation of Israel under the Old Testament economy. This can be illustrated by the use of the Old Testament text of 2 Chronicles 7:14, which is often used as though it applies literally to the United States of America, as it did to Israel of the Old Testament.

There is a sense in which the people of God of New Testament persuasion have as much right to use this text as do Old Testament people; after all, everything about the Christian faith comes out of Old Testament faith. The roots of Christian faith are Jewish. Our Saviour and Lord was Jewish. Except for Doctor Luke, the writers of the New Testament were Jewish. In fact, one of my great concerns as a pastor over the last 20 years is the fact that we seem to be losing the Jewishness in our faith.

Furthermore, the promise is addressed to the people of God, the people who are called by His name. Blessing is promised to those who meet the conditions that God laid down in this very important text. One thing is clear from the text, and that is that God deals with His people when He wants to bless a land or a nation. God does not bypass His people, bringing blessing in spite of them. He works through His people, and when His people meet the conditions laid down in this remarkable promise, they can expect that blessings will accrue, not only to themselves but to their total environment.

When the people of God are salty, they enhance the life of their environment, making it more palatable. They are a preservative force in their environment. They make a great difference when they conform to God's will for them. When they are light in a dark world, God is glorified and the larger community is blessed.

In this general sense, all of us have a right to take 2 Chronicles 7:14 personally and to expect the blessings of God on our land when we conform. But the land to be healed is not to be equated with the land as it was understood in the Old Testament.

God has certainly blessed the United States as no other modern nation and her influence in the modern world has been immeasurable in many godly ways, but there is no biblical justification for assuming that God has a special plan to save the United States any more than any other nation—the Soviet Union, for example. The idea, which not uncommonly surfaces by implication rather than verbally, is that if we can get Christians into places of power—the White House, Congress, Supreme Court, etc.—we will have the Kingdom of God on earth. This view cannot be supported by Scripture.

This does not mean that we should not pray and work that our nation may be as righteous and strong and free and powerful as possible, but it does mean that the Kingdom of God, which is here and is coming, is not to be confused with the "good old U.S.A."

Some years ago Malcolm Muggeridge of England was a guest of a number of men at a prayer breakfast in Washington, D.C. He gave his personal testimony concerning what he calls his "rediscovery of Jesus," after which he spoke off-the-cuff concerning world conditions. Those who know Malcolm Muggeridge know that he tends to be very pessimistic. He is probably one of the best-informed men in the world, and when he speaks of world conditions, he is pessimistic.

When he finished his remarks he asked for questions or comments. The first question was, "Brother Muggeridge, you have been very pessimistic this morning. Isn't there anything about which you are optimistic?"

Dr. Muggeridge responded, "My brother, I couldn't be more optimistic than I am, because my hope is solely and alone in Jesus

Christ and His triumph in history." For a brief moment there was heavy silence. Then Malcolm Muggeridge dropped this bombshell on the group. "Just imagine if the apostolic church had pinned its hope on the Roman Empire."[11]

One senses today, in a great deal that is said and done in terms of government and public policy and protest, that there is an unverbalized assumption that somehow the Kingdom of God can be built in the United States in such a way that the time will arrive when this nation will actually become the Kingdom of God on earth, even though Jesus said His Kingdom was not of this world.

During the church/state debate previous to the 1984 presidential elections I received a good deal of mail, often angry mail. It made me wonder—What if the only identity of the follower of Christ was the quality of his or her life? What if there were no religious institutions, no religious labels? What if the words Catholic, Protestant, Jew, Presbyterian, Methodist, Baptist, Episcopalian, etc., were unknown? What if the only way a follower of Christ could be identified in the world was by the Christlikeness of his or her life? Because, in the final analysis, that is the fundamental, the essential witness to Christ in the world.

As a matter of fact, the most effective witness to Christ in the world in history can be understood by the distinction between two little words: *in* and *on*. The influence of the Church of Jesus Christ *on* organizations from without is infinitesimal compared to the influence of Jesus Christ from *within* these institutions. The witness from within is infinitely more effective than the witness from without.

This is not to demean the influence of the Church on the various organizations and institutions or to ignore the influence from

*Our country was founded on religious freedom. Various types of places of worship abound across our land. But what if we didn't have these physical places of worship or our "religious tags" to identify our faith? What if the only identity of the follower of Christ was the quality of his or her life?*

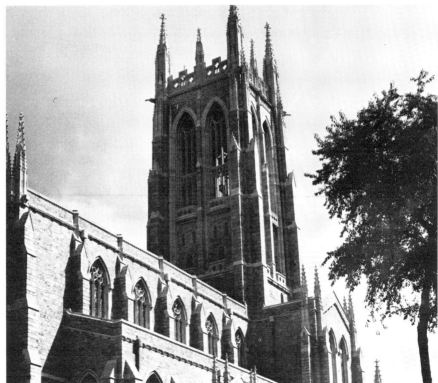

Photographs by Harold M. Lambert

without. It is to recognize the reality that is so often forgotten, namely, that while church institutions and various organizations are attempting to influence government from without by their proclamations, their programs, their protests, and their resolutions, within the government there are literally thousands of followers of Jesus Christ going about their daily tasks with a sense of having been placed there by Christ, accountable to Him to live their lives and do their tasks to the glory of God. There is no way to measure this influence from within, but it is certainly undeniable that this is the way of Christ.

In the Sermon on the Mount following the beatitudes, Jesus referred to His disciples as "salt of the earth" and "light of the world." In His parables of the Kingdom found in Matthew 13, He referred to the children of the Kingdom as the good seed, which the sower, Jesus Christ, plants in the field, which is the world. He describes the Kingdom as leaven in another parable.

All four of these images have something in common: they work from within. Salt penetrates the food. Light penetrates the darkness. Seed penetrates the soil. Leaven penetrates the lump. When these forces are at work within they are invisible. So it is with the Church of Jesus Christ, the people of God.

The fact is that there are thousands of faithful servants of Christ working within government. They are not there by accident. They have been planted there by Jesus Christ as good seed in the soil of government. What better place for a servant of Christ to be serving Him? What more effective way to influence the world for Christ?

On the occasion of the annual convention of the National Association of Christian Educators in Washington, D.C., I was asked to speak at one of their meetings at breakfast. In preparing for that event, I learned that there are 300,000 servants of Jesus Christ teaching in public schools. With those statistics in mind and in the context of what has just been said in the foregoing paragraph, I prepared my talk.

When I arrived at the breakfast I was escorted to the table

where the president and some of the other officers sat. Wanting to be very sure of my statistics, I asked the president if they were right. He said, as a matter of fact, that they were probably very conservative. He estimated that there were 500,000 Christian teachers in the public school systems of America.

I began my remarks with those statistics and then asked the question, "What do you think the Soviet Union would do if it had 500,000 hard-core, card-carrying Communists teaching in the public school systems of the United States?"

Then I suggested two things they would not do. They would not declare themselves to be Communists. They would do everything in their power to keep that a secret. They would do everything in their power to infiltrate with their charm and their ideology. Their influence would be subversive. (By the way, the influence of the Church of Jesus Christ in history is not so much that of an army marching with banners flying and bands playing; it is more like benevolent subversion, like a secret service infiltrating the enemy.)

The second thing I said the Communists would not do would be to start Communist schools. Their strategy would be to penetrate, to make disciples and to recruit for the Communist cause. Remember Satan's master strategy is his incognito.

It must not be implied from the above that I oppose Christian schools. I am, in fact, a product of a great Christian college, and I encourage and support the whole Christian school emphasis. But it should be obvious that the only non-Christians that can be influenced by a Christian school are those who attend the Christian school until, of course, the graduates of the Christian school take their place in the world and penetrate its institutions. The tragedy of this is that if we abandon the public school system, we are, in effect, surrendering to the enemy and sacrificing one of the most fundamental opportunities to be an influence for Jesus Christ in the world.

We evangelicals tend to do this. We withdraw the best and godliest of our sisters and brothers in Christ out of contact with the world and, in so doing, we abandon the organizations and institutions to godless leadership and godless influence. All the time we are protesting secularism and humanism we are surrendering to the very influence we decry.

This is the consummate strategy of God's redemptive purpose in history. Generally speaking, God's influence, that is, His self-revelation or self-disclosure up until the time of Jesus Christ, was an influence *on* the world. The birth of Jesus Christ represented God's entrance into the world—into human history—into the human family.

In writing to the Galatians, the Apostle Paul put it this way: "But when the time had fully come, God sent his Son, born of a woman, born under law" (Galatians 4:4). The reference to time in this situation is significant. Paul is writing, of course, from the standpoint of an eternal God for whom a thousand years is as a day. Note the schedule, "When the time had fully come." In the economy of God, "the time had fully come" when Jesus Christ was born. One senses God's sovereign overrule of time in history in this clause. From the standpoint of God's redemptive program in history, time had fully come with the birth of Jesus Christ.

The author of Hebrews opens his epistle with these words: "In the past God spoke to our forefathers through the prophets at many times and in various ways, but in these last days he has spoken to us by his Son" (Hebrews 1:1-2). Note again the reference to divine timing or schedule: "in these last days." In terms of God's redemptive plan in history, the last days began with the advent of Jesus Christ into the world, or, to put it another way, we have been living in the fullness of time for 2,000 years. The world has been in these last days all that time.

One might think of it this way. In the final phase of His redemptive plan, God has been moving from within history, within the human family, within time. God continues outside of history, outside of the world, outside of time. That is to say He is transcendant; but since the incarnation of Jesus Christ, He is now working inside. He is immanent. He is the omnipresent God, which means

He exists everywhere at once. There is nowhere He is not.

In the prologue to his gospel, the Apostle John wrote, "Without him nothing was made that has been made. In him was life, and that life was the light of men" (John 1:3-4). In verse 14 of the same chapter, John writes, "The Word became flesh and lived for a while among us. We have seen his glory, the glory of the one and only Son, who came from the Father, full of grace and truth."

The word had been *outside* from the beginning. Now the word is *in* flesh (incarnate) and dwells *in* our midst. In this Word made flesh—that is, Jesus Christ—exists the incarnate Son of God. Heretofore, God had revealed Himself in creation, in nature, in the physical and moral order, in history through Israel and the prophets.

Jesus, in His high priestly intercession to His Father, prayed, "For they are not of the world any more than I am of the world. My prayer is not that you take them out of the world but that you protect them from the evil one. As you sent me into the world, I have sent them into the world" (John 17:14,15,18). As the Father has sent the Son into the world as the final and supreme revelation of Himself within human history, now the Son was to send His disciples into the world as His witnesses within history. The supreme witness, the supreme impact of God upon the world was to be from within.

The Apostle Paul presents this graphically in his letter to the Philippians. He wrote, "Your attitude should be the same as that of Christ Jesus: Who, being in very nature God, did not consider equality with God something to be grasped, but made himself nothing, taking the very nature of a servant, being made in human likeness. And being found in appearance as a man, he humbled himself and became obedient to death—even death on a cross!" (Philippians 2:5-8).

This is the point. God's final, supreme self-witness to the world is from *within* the world—from *within* the human race—for the sake of the redemption of humanity. So Christ sends His people into the world of medicine, law, construction, business, architecture, agriculture, government, education, the home, society, etc., that from *within* His glory might be beheld.

As the Son prayed so compassionately to the Father for those He had sent into the world, so ought we to support with our supplications the salt, the light, the good seed, the leaven by which Jesus Christ penetrates all the structures and institutions of the world. Every servant of Christ is in the world some place. He is not there by accident. He was sent there by his Saviour and Lord. He should accept his being there as the purpose of God for his life.

Oswald Chambers in his devotional book, *My Utmost for His Highest,* has a sentence that puts all of this into perspective. He writes, "Never allow the thought 'I am of no use where I am.' You are certainly of no use where you are not."

It is not an afterthought to suggest that, if we could have seen into the minds of our founding fathers, we would realize that they probably did not envision the professional politician. Their vision was that of the common citizen being involved in the political process, while at the same time supporting himself with his own trade or profession or business. We have long since removed ourselves from that vision and intention of our forbears, and it is unrealistic to think that we could ever return to it. Our government has grown in ways that are endemic in its origins, even if our founding fathers did not envision our particular kind of growth.

As believers seek to know the mind of Christ and the plan of God for their lives in various vocations, professions and careers, it is not unreasonable to suggest that, in the process, they ought to consider the possibility of a term in public office. The door to one's life should be kept open to such a possibility. Young men and women in the process of their education certainly ought to consider public life or elective office as one of the possible careers God may have chosen for them. Assuming that a servant of Jesus Christ is qualified and has the credentials, there is no more effective avenue of ministry than public service.

In his letter to the Romans, the Apostle Paul indicates that government service, or public service, is as much a ministry of

God as any other ministry that one can think of. He writes:

*Everyone must submit himself to the governing authorities, for there is no authority except that which God has established. The authorities that exist have been established by God. Consequently, he who rebels against the authority is rebelling against what God has instituted, and those who do so will bring judgment on themselves. For rulers hold no terror for those who do right, but for those who do wrong. Do you want to be free from fear of the one in authority? Then do what is right and he will commend you. For he is God's servant to do you good. But if you do wrong, be afraid, for he does not bear the sword for nothing. He is God's servant, an agent of wrath to bring punishment on the wrongdoer. Therefore, it is necessary to submit to the authorities, not only because of possible punishment but also because of conscience. This is also why you pay taxes, for the authorities are God's servants, who give their full time to governing. Give everyone what you owe him: If you owe taxes, pay taxes; if revenue, then revenue; if respect, then respect, if honor, then honor"* (Romans 13:1-7).

Public servants are God's servants. Why should government service or political life be any less a challenge to the world mission than the conventional pastorate or the missionary overseas?

CHAPTER 5

# The Peril in Prosperity

D uring the 43 years Doris and I have been married, I have, on very rare special occasions, purchased an orchid corsage for her; the ritual, when she receives the corsage, is always the same. She wears it for the event. Then, when we come home that evening, she carefully places the corsage in the cotton batten, sprinkles some water on it, and puts it in the refrigerator. She wants to preserve the beauty and fragrance of that orchid as long as she can, and wear it as often as possible. Both of us know, however, that regardless of how careful she is, the fragrance and beauty of that orchid cannot be preserved indefinitely because it has been cut from its roots—it is lifeless. Sooner or later, it must be consigned to the trash can.

It is my conviction, after living in Washington, D.C. for 30 years, that this is precisely where we are at this moment in our national life. More than five years in the Senate confirms this conviction. Frustration is compounding as powerful people, civil and religious, do everything they possibly can in a futile effort to preserve the order, beauty and goodness of our land. Instead of improving, circumstances get worse. America has become detached from its spiritual and moral roots.

It was my hope, as we approached the bicentennial of our nation, that we would see a difference. Millions across the nation hoped, felt, worked, and prayed that the bicentennial would draw us back to the virtues and values that had made us great. It didn't happen.

Now, as we celebrate the bicentennial of our Constitution, we have another great opportunity to consider our national legacy and the foundation upon which we've built—a foundation from which, if we are detached, there simply is no hope of preserving the greatness of America.

Last year, in the rotunda of the Capitol, there was a celebration receiving Anatoly Scharansky, who had just been released earlier from a Russian prison. It was a great event at which Senator Bob Dole, the majority leader, Senator Robert Byrd, the Democratic leader, and Speaker Tip O'Neill reminded us that this liberated man had been the victim of a godless government. Human rights mean nothing in Russia because it is a godless government. When you take God out of politics, human rights are meaningless. Government becomes sovereign instead of people and human rights are decided by government. Our system will not work if we reject a Creator God.

In an editorial dated September 22, 1986, on the occasion of the imprisonment by the Soviets of Nicholas Daniloff, chairman and editor in chief of *U.S. News and World Report,* Mortimer B. Zuckerman, wrote: "Americans have been outraged by the imprisonment of Nicholas Daniloff, but there has been bewilderment with the anger. Why should Gorbachev risk his campaign for arms control by such an offense? Didn't he anticipate our reaction? The bafflement arises because we assume the Soviets inhabit the same moral universe. They don't. It was the same with Chernobyl. How could the Soviets delay warning neighboring states and lie to them?

"The answer is twofold. In the Soviet system, the perceived interests of the state are paramount. A society that does not cherish the individual has no scruples holding any individual hostage.

Secondly, there is ignorance of public reaction. The Soviet Union is, as we know, a closed society, without a free press, where leaders do not have to justify themselves to public opinion. Totalitarian leaders who do not have to respond democratically to their own people are insulated. Their isolation is compounded by centuries of hostility to and paranoia about foreigners. Thus, they are prone to miscalculate in dealings with other countries.

"The contrasts could not be greater. The Soviet Union has never known a day of democratic freedom in its history. The United States was conceived and developed as the most open society in the free world. An energetic free press provides regular feedback on public reaction. Both societies have ambitions to be the dominant world power. But the U.S., though passionate for the advancement of freedom in the world, is satisfied with peaceful, evolutionary change while the U.S.S.R. is a dissatisfied imperial power, revolutionary in its ideological outlook, expansionist in its historic urges."[12]

Fifteen hundred years before Christ—3,500 years ago—Moses, the mighty prophet and deliverer, was preparing the Old Testament people for their entrance into the land of promise. They had wandered 40 years in the wilderness. Moses himself, because of disobedience, would not be allowed to enter. God allowed him to see the land from a distance, but it was up to his successor, Joshua, to lead the people in. Now they are gathered at Kadesh Barnea, where they had been 38½ years before and had not been permitted to enter.

The book of Deuteronomy contains Moses' instructions to the Old Testament people of God, preparing them for their entrance. In the course of his instruction, he gave them this warning:

*Be careful that you do not forget the Lord your God, failing to observe his commands . . . . Otherwise, when you eat and are satisfied, when you build fine houses and settle down, and when your herds and flocks grow large and your silver and gold increase and all you have is multiplied, then your heart will become proud and you will forget the Lord your God* (Deuteronomy 8:11-14).

What a significant statement from the mouth of the great prophet, Moses, demonstrating the unity, continuity and solidarity of biblical truth. Moses understood the peril in prosperity. He understood how easily wealth can replace God in our lives.

It is important to note here that Moses is not critical of prosperity. He is not criticizing the wealthy nor intimating that wealth is wrong. On the contrary, a few sentences later in his instruction he makes it clear that God gives the power to get wealth. The point is not that wealth is wrong, but that, if it replaces God, it is destructive.

Moses' warning continues: *You may say to yourself, "My power and the strength of my hands have produced this wealth for me." But remember the Lord your God, for it is he who gives you the ability to produce wealth . . . . If you ever forget the Lord your God and follow other gods and worship and bow down to them, I testify against you today that you will surely be destroyed. Like the nations the Lord destroyed before you, so you will be destroyed for not obeying the Lord your God* (Deuteronomy 8:17-20).

Jesus understood this principle. He said, "No one can serve two masters. Either he will hate the one and love the other, or he will be devoted to the one and despise the other. You cannot serve both God and Money" (Matthew 6:24). You cannot serve both God and money. You will serve one or the other. If money is your god, beware.

In the book of Revelation, the Lord speaks to the seven churches of the revelation. The last word is to the church of Laodicea. There is a tradition in biblical teaching and church history that not only were those seven churches real churches in the time of the writing of the book of Revelation, they also represent seven periods of church history. Teaching suggests (and I am not defending the view) that we are in the Laodicean period, the last period of church history. Now what was God's message to the church at Laodicea?

*I know your deeds, that you are neither cold nor hot. I wish you were either one or the other! So, because you are lukewarm—neither hot nor cold—I am about to spit you out of my mouth* (Revelation 3:15,16).

Lukewarmness makes God want to vomit; it is intolerable to Him.

One of my favorite friends for many years (he is in heaven now), Roger Hull, president of Mutual of New York, used to say as he would travel around the country speaking to laymen, "The greatest danger we face in America today is the casual Christian."

What are the symptoms of lukewarmness? *You say, "I am rich; I have acquired wealth and do not need a thing." But you do not realize that you are wretched, pitiful, poor, blind and naked* (Revelation 3:17).

Need is the growing edge of life. You eat because you're hungry; you drink because you're thirsty; you rest because you're weary. A corpse doesn't have any needs. If you do not have any needs, you're dead. You grow by need and the Laodicean church was lukewarm. It needed nothing because it was rich and increased with goods. The peril of prosperity! God gave His estimate of that same church: "But you do not realize that you are wretched, pitiful, poor, blind and naked." God's estimate of the lukewarm church is quite opposite its own self-perception. And that is the peril of prosperity.

In 1863 President Lincoln proclaimed a day of national humiliation, fasting and prayer. In his proclamation, he wrote, "It is the duty of nations as well as of men to owe their dependence on the overruling power of God, to confess their sins and transgressions in humble sorrow, yet with assured hope that genuine repentance will lead to mercy and pardon and to recognize the sublime truth announced in the Holy Scriptures and proven by all history that those nations only are blessed whose God is the Lord. The awful calamity of Civil War which now desolates the land may be but a punishment inflicted upon us for our presumptuous sins, the needful end of our national reformation as a whole people. Intoxicated

Above: *"When Abraham Lincoln Took the Oath of Office."* President Lincoln, a deeply religious man, proclaimed a day of national humiliation, fasting and prayer in 1863.

Right: *Thousands of visitors to Washington, D.C., stop to view this statue of Abraham Lincoln and to pay their respects to the slain president who reminded us of our need for dependence upon God.*

IN THIS TEMPLE
AS IN THE HEARTS OF THE PEOPLE
FOR WHOM HE SAVED THE UNION
THE MEMORY OF ABRAHAM LINCOLN
IS ENSHRINED FOREVER

with unbroken success, we have become too self-sufficient to feel the necessity of redeeming and preserving grace, too proud to pray to the Lord, God, that made us. We have grown in numbers, wealth, and power, as no other nation has grown, but we have forgotten God. We have forgotten the gracious hand that preserved us in peace and multiplied and enriched and strengthened us. We have vainly imagined that all these blessings were produced by some superior virtue and wisdom of our own. It behooves us then to humble ourselves and confess our national sins and to pray for clemency and forgiveness."[13]

In *Life Magazine,* dated April 11, 1949, a center spread editorial went as follows: "Communism is not the only threat to Western civilization and perhaps not the greatest threat. The greatest threat to our civilization comes from within that civilization itself. Our $64 euphemism for it is secularism. A much blunter word is godlessness. Our civilization for all its churches and churchgoers is predominantly a secular, godless civilization."[14]

*Secular* is not a bad word. The dichotomy so commonly made between the secular and the sacred or the spiritual is a false dichotomy. It is not a biblical dichotomy. Everything that exists comes from God. God created the secular world. It is recorded at the end of Genesis 1 that God saw all that He had created and it was "very good." Christ sends His people into a secular world where He expects them to live as Kingdom of God people, doing all they can do to the glory of God and permeating their environment with Kingdom of God quality and life and conditions.

Secularism is a condition in which God is organized out of life. Secularism denies the spiritual, the supernatural, the eternal, the invisible realities of life. Secularism is the product of which secularization is the process. Secularization has at least two perilous results in a culture. It forces religious faith out of public life, and it materializes a society. As God becomes less and less important, less and less relevant to people, materialism becomes more and more the sole reality. As the process of secularization advances, material things become increasingly important. Religious faith—

belief in God—becomes less important. Intellectual or philosophical atheism may not replace religious faith, and a belief in God may continue, but life is lived as though God were nonexistent—as though belief in God is simply a matter of indifference.

Eugene Thomas Long, in the book, *God, Secularization and History,* defines secularization as a "worldly view of reality—a concern with the world in which man lives and makes his own being and a rejection of a dualistic view of reality with its other view of timeless truth."[15]

One of the most influential men in Washington for many years was David Lawrence, the founder and editor at the time of the *U.S. News and World Report.* He was the only nonsenator, apart from those of us involved in the Prayer Breakfast Movement, who attended the Senate prayer breakfasts. He was often asked to speak and always drew a large attendance. In an editorial dated May 25, 1956, he wrote, "It is a temporary answer to the threat of world disturbance that we face. The North Atlantic Treaty is temporary. The United Nations are temporary. All our alliances are temporary. Basically, there is only one permanence we can all accept. It is the permanence of a God-governed world. For the power of God alone is permanent. Obedience to his law is the only road to lasting solutions to man's problems."[16]

On the deck of the battleship *Missouri,* when he signed the peace with Japan, General of the Army Douglas MacArthur said this: "Military alliances, balances of power, leagues of nations, all in turn have failed, leaving the only path to be by the crucible of war. The utter destructiveness of war now blocks out this alternative. We have had our last chance. If we do not devise some greater and more equitable system, Armageddon will be at our door. The problem is *basically theological,* and involves a spiritual recrudescence and improvement of human character that will synchronize with our almost matchless advance in science, art, etc., over the past 2,000 years. It *must be of the spirit if we are to save the flesh*"[17] (italics mine).

As you walk into the Jefferson Memorial just off the Tidal Basin in Washington, D.C., on the right hand wall is inscribed that whole paragraph from which I quoted earlier, "We hold these truths to be self-evident . . . " As you walk out of the Memorial to the right, when you're facing the Tidal Basin, there is a long paragraph containing two sentences, the first of which is a categorical statement, the second, a penetrating question.

I would like to suggest that it is incumbent upon each American to face this penetrating question asked by Thomas Jefferson, and answer it for himself, for herself. To avoid this question makes one a part of the problem, not part of the solution. The first sentence is this: "God who gave us life, gave us liberty." The question: "Can the liberties of a nation be secure when we have removed the conviction that these liberties are the gift of God?"[18]

What do you think? When the angel of the Lord spoke to the church at Laodicea, he described its problem and prescribed its cure: "Here I am! I stand at the door and knock. If anyone hears my voice and opens the door, I will come in and eat with him, and he with me" (Revelations 3:20). This is God's answer to the peril of prosperity. This is the answer to Jefferson's question. This is the only hope we have as a nation.

For Moses, 1500 years before Christ, for General of the Army Douglas MacArthur, 45 years ago, we have the same diagnosis of the problem, implicit in which is the remedy, the cure. The American political system is based upon the proposition that God created humans equal, that He endowed them with certain inalienable rights, that government is to secure these rights, and that it receives its just authority from the people it governs.

In other words, our system is built upon the sovereignty of the people based upon a Creator God. If God is forsaken, the system will ultimately collapse. Is it not conceivable that the reason the

*Each year thousands of American citizens visit the Jefferson Memorial. It is a tribute to the author of the Declaration of Independence and third president of the United States. The following inscription occupies the frieze of the main entablature: "I have sworn upon the altar of God eternal hostility against every form of tyranny over the mind of man."*

81

people in the United States have abdicated their sovereignty is because, in the midst of our prosperity, we have forgotten the God who makes the system work?

In a letter dated July 29, 1986, written to Chuck Colson, founder and chairman of the board of the Prison Fellowship, Dennis F. Kinlaw, president of the Francis Asbury Society, Wilmore, Kentucky, wrote: "It is my belief that you and Prison Fellowship represent what may well be the most significant witness for the Lord in this secular culture of ours. The church by and large has forfeited its role as a voice of God. *Most of evangelicalism has an in-house witness that the world can ignore, because the world sees its motivation as completely comprehensible and consonant with its own.* The incomprehensibility to the natural man of the true witness, like that which Moses experienced when the bush burned but was not consumed, is absent. It is not surprising that the world does not turn to wonder.

"Prison fellowship is different. It runs counter to all our natural inclinations. It gets at what only grace can give. The witness to the biblical demand for justice and the reality of agape love is clearer there, or so it seems to me, than anywhere else in our society"[19] (italics mine).

Earlier in this book some comments were made regarding a very familiar text, often quoted in evangelical circles. I refer to 2 Chronicles 7:14. "If my people, who are called by my name, will humble themselves and pray and seek my face and turn from their wicked ways, then will I hear from heaven and will forgive their sin and will heal their land." One wonders at a strange anomaly that has occurred in our national life. In the past four or five decades, at a time when the biblical term *born again* has become almost popular, certainly very common; when there has been an extraordinary resurgence of evangelicalism, when evangelicals are receiving more press and publicity than perhaps at any other time in our history; when evangelical publishers are becoming big business; when evangelical television preachers are reaching tens of millions daily—at the same time social evils such as divorce, battered wives, abused children, chemical dependence, pornography, and crime have been increasing in epidemic proportions.

That well known Scripture, 2 Chronicles 7:14, has certainly been quoted innumerable times. People of God have sought God's face. They have humbled themselves. They have prayed. What has prevented the healing of the land as God has promised?

Is it possible that the clue is found in the final condition set forth by God, "turn from their wicked ways"? When we read this term or hear it, what comes to mind? Do we think of personal immoral practices, from which we who profess Christ are quite willing to turn? Is it possible that the wicked ways to which God refers in the promise is the wickedness to which Moses referred in his warning to the Israelites—the wickedness of materialism, the wickedness of secularism? In our prosperity and power, have we evangelicals been so totally infected by materialism that we are oblivious to the very evil or wickedness from which our heavenly Father urges us to turn?

We are part of a success-oriented culture and we have been badly infected with the passion for success. Do we not hear our Lord Jesus Christ when He says, "Do not store up for yourselves treasures on earth, where moth and rust destroy, and where thieves break in and steal. But store up for yourselves treasures in heaven, where moth and rust do not destroy, and where thieves do not break in and steal" (Matthew 6:19-20)? Do we not hear the categorical and clear command of our Lord Jesus Christ as He says, "Seek first his kingdom and his righteousness" (Matthew 6:33)? Should we not heed the warning of Moses to the Israelites; the indictment of the Lord to the church of Laodicea; the passion-ate proclamation of President Lincoln calling the nation to a day of national humiliation, fasting and prayer; the *Life Magazine* editorial; the wise counsel of David Lawrence in his editorial; the words of General MacArthur on the deck of the battleship *Missouri*?

Is God waiting for His Church—His people—to repudiate materialism as a way of life before He visits our land with purify-ing, cleansing, renewing power?

God of Abraham, Isaac and Israel, yesterday we celebrated
the heroism of a very uncommon man, Natan (Anatoly)
Scharansky, whose indomitable spirit was unyielding
against incredibly powerful pressures. Despite innumerable threats
and enticements, he did not stop worshiping his God. We were
reminded that he was the victim of a godless government. Mighty
God, help us to hear this! May his experience engrave in our minds
the fact that when godlessness is official government policy, human
rights are a matter of indifference.

As we celebrated, Heavenly Father, two sentences enshrined in
the Jefferson Memorial came to mind: "God who gave us life, gave
us liberty. Can the liberties of a nation be secure when we have
removed the conviction that these liberties are the gift of God?" Help
us, Dear God, never to forget or ignore this profound conviction of
our founding fathers that human rights are inalienable because
they are endowed by Creator God. Save us, Lord, from the sacrifice
of all we hold dear by removing the conviction human rights are the
gift of God. Grant us grace to resist with all our being a godless
political system. In your matchless name we pray,
Amen.

Prayer in the Senate, May 14, 1986

# Appendices

# An Introduction to the Constitution of the United States

INTRODUCTION BY MERRILL EDWARD GATES, LL.D., L.H.D.

Every one who values his property can give some account of his own possessions. You know what you own. You mean to keep clear your title to it. Every true American values his own personal rights and his political freedom even more highly than he values his property. Our forefathers, 130 years ago, made an instrument designed to protect their rights and ours. "To establish Justice," and maintain fair treatment and an equal opportunity for all; "to promote the general Welfare and secure the Blessings of Liberty to ourselves and our Posterity," is our wish, our national will, our steadfast purpose as true Americans, now, as it was four generations ago when great Americans founded our government.

### The Title-Deed of Freedom

The Constitution of the United States is the *workingman's charter to protect his personal liberty.* It is the title-deed by which each one of us holds his personal freedom, his property, and his right to home and to the family life which is dear to us all. If you own your home, if you have a title to a piece of land and a house, you take care of your title-deed. You know well what the title is worth to you, and you value it. Once in a while you read it over. You take care not to lose

it! We have, each one of us Americans, a title-deed to a share in the blessings of the best government in the world. And the great fundamental law of that government, the Constitution of the United States, every citizen of the United States ought to know. Every citizen ought to have a copy of it within reach. Have you ever studied your title-deed to all the rights of an American—the Constitution? How long since you read it through?

In these months, when so many millions of people are suffering and dying for lack of a stable government of just laws, well administered, you ought to refresh your memory by reading again, and again giving thanks for those guarantees of justice, personal freedom and equal rights which are given you in that fundamental law of our land, "The Constitution." All the people should know it and defend it, for it was made and it is maintained by our "sovereign power, the people of the United States;" and you are one of these people.

### Stability and Growth

If a person has lived in good health for a hundred years, we say, "he has a good constitution." The Constitution of the United States has been in successful operation now for more than

The above is from the Pocket Edition of *The Constitution of the United States with an Introduction by Merrill E. Gates, LL.D., L.H.D.,* formerly president of Rutgers College, later president of Amherst College, published by The National Association for Constitutional Government, Washington, D.C., 1919.

a hundred and thirty years. Ours is the oldest republic among the great self-governing states of the world. Under our Constitution we have grown, from a little experimental republic of four millions, to be a world-power of a hundred and ten millions. The great Americans who planned our government were wise and far-seeing, and they gave us a foundation-law which has the surest promise of continued life, a constitution founded on principles of justice that are stable and unchanging, like the solid earth under our feet; yet a constitution which within itself provides for change and growth to meet the needs of expanding life. It can be amended. It has been amended whenever the people of the United States became deliberately convinced that a change was needed. Yet our Constitution, like other living and growing things, changes not by a stroke—not by a revolution or a threat—but by the deliberate growth of a conviction on the part of the great mass of the people, a conviction which expresses itself in the methods provided for by the Constitution itself, so that successive amendments as required by the people may always insure to us a government "deriving its just powers from the consent of the governed."

It is this great basal law of our land, it is the Constitution, that secures to every working-man the wages he earns, the savings he has made and invested, the home and the property he has acquired and owns. That "fair opportunity for every one," that "equality before the law," which is our American boast and birthright, is secured to us by the Constitution.

## The "State" and "Government"

To enforce and maintain justice, there must be a government, based on law, and obeying law. Every state must have a government.

The word "state" means something stable, something that stands, endures. The state is "society organized to maintain justice." It is society stabilized—kept steady—established—not whirling in socialistic anarchy, like Russia in 1918-19—not overturned in ceaseless revolutions, even if revolutionists do profess to aim at liberty. An established government must have definite organs provided for in its fundamental law—offices, and officers through whom the state acts in governing—in maintaining order and administering justice. Order and justice must be maintained not at one man's caprice, or by one man's will, but by uniform laws applicable to all. Whatever name may be given to a state, its government must have definite organs for each of the three great branches of the state's activity: the Legislative (to make the laws), the Executive (to execute and administer the laws), and the Judiciary (courts and judges to interpret and apply the laws and the principles of justice to the particular cases that arise). Emperors and Kings who claim absolute sovereign power and authority for their own arbitrary will, the world has done with! But every independent state must have sovereign power and exclusive authority over a definite territory—a distinctly bounded portion of the earth's surface. And every state that endures long enough to have a name and a place among the states of the world, must have a definite form of government in which these three essential functions of government are fixed, and their form and their functions defined, in a constitution, written or unwritten.

## The Fundamental Law of the State

Our Constitution is the great, basal, fundamental law of the State, which defines the objects of good government, and fixes the form and defines the powers of the organs of government. At the same time, it secures to the individual his rights as against any attempted aggression by the government. All the officers of our government, from the highest to the lowest, must swear allegiance to the Constitution; and they all depend upon the Constitution for their authority. All their powers are derived from the Constitution. In all self-governing nations of the world, the *fundamental law, the constitution, derives its authority and its power from the people.* Other laws are made by the legislative bodies which have been created for that purpose by the Constitution. But the Constitution itself is the work and the sovereign will of the people. "We the people of the United States"—(and not the several states or their legislatures)—"we the people of the" whole "United States * * * do ordain and establish this Constitution for the United States of America," said our people when they founded our Government. And all the changes that have been made in our fundamental Organic Law by the nineteen amendments adopted since 1789, have been made by the sovereign people of the United States. Always our government has rested upon the will of the people as expressed in our Constitution.

## Government by and for the People

It is not too much to say that the whole civilized world has now adopted as the basis of government the sentences from the Declaration of Independence which in 1776 preceded our Constitution. All progressive nations now hold that "instituted among men to secure certain inalienable rights" such as "life, liberty and the pursuit of happiness"—"governments derive their just powers from the consent of the governed."

Why do we in the United States not live in constant fear of revolution? Because our government, our Constitution, expresses the will of the people, is the work of the people, and can be amended as the deliberate and intelligent convictions of the people call for changes and enact amendments. Why should our people fear revolution, when with us the majority rules, and rules under the authority of a Constitution which more than a mere majority of the people have made and approved, and can amend? Why should our people ever desire a revolution, while our Constitution provides for a peaceful and orderly method for correcting abuses of power or infringements of rights? We have, already, the liberty which oppressed peoples rebel in order to attain. We have that "government by the people" in accordance with laws of their own making through their chosen representatives, which expresses the just will of a self-determining people.

The Constitution is the foundation of our Government. As the foundation of a house, or of any large building, is so laid out as to bear the weight and sustain the strain of the building which it underlies and upholds, the foundation is a kind of ground-plan or outline of the superstructure. Just so, the constitution of a state is the enduring, not easily changed foundation-law which gives shape and stability to the state, and defines and limits the form, the function and the powers of each of the organs of that state. The state is always "society jurally organized,"—"society organized to maintain justice."

## Democracy Built Upon Justice

What is justice? Who can give a better definition than the one given by the Roman Law in Ulpian's words: *Constans et perpetua voluntas jus suum cuique tribuendi;"* that is, "the steadfast, unchanging will and purpose to give to every one his due." It gives confidence, to feel that for two thousand years the leaders of civilization, from the men of Athens and Rome to the founders of our Constitution and the men in khaki of our own time, who have been ready to give their lives to defend this idea of justice— that through all these centuries, the leaders of the world's civilization have held steadily to this idea of justice, which has been once more gloriously vindicated by the war just closing. Our Constitution makes it possible for us in the United States to say and to feel: "Here in America every man has a fair chance, and knows that he has it." And that is true, free democracy. That means justice and freedom for all. That spirit, worked out in law and maintained in administration, is the essence of the true democracy which it is safe for the world to profess and to practice.

To preserve liberty, there must be voluntary and intelligent obedience to law. To insure the administration of justice by a state, there must always be a fundamental law, a constitution that defines and stabilizes government. For the peoples of those lands which are fragments of the broken empires of Austria and Turkey— for the Balkan States and the newly created republics in Europe, as well as for distracted Russia,—a constitution wisely framed and heartily accepted by the people of each state, is still the great need.

## Constitutions and the Will of the Majority

In the eighteenth and nineteenth centuries, the peoples of Europe were demanding constitutions to protect them against the exactions and injustice of kings and emperors. Now, *constitutions are needed* and are demanded in many parts of Europe and Asia, not so much to limit kings and emperors, as *to make sure that when the people rule themselves, they shall rule in justice and without tyrannical abuse of power by the majority.* In democracies and republics, no less than in monarchies, personal rights and property rights need to be recognized and the organs and methods of government need to be defined in the fundamental law, in constitutions; and these rights of all the people need to be respected and maintained in administrative government. No state, whether monarchy, empire, democracy or republic, can exist and hold a place among the nations of the earth, without the accepted reign of law. No free state can exist without the voluntary acceptance by the people of self-imposed obedience to law—to moral law and to enacted law. Lawlessness is not liberty! Anarchy is not freedom! No freedom is possible except under the reign of law. "A fundamental law forbidding class, sectional and inspirational legislation, is the indispensable guarantee of personal liberty, and the necessary basis of true social justice." The most abject and terrible slavery the world has even known has been the tyranny of lawless majorities in the exercise of unlimited power. Witness the "reign of terror" during the French Revolution, and the tyrannical class "autocracy of the proletariat" dominated by the bolshevist socialists, Lenine and Trotzky! With us in the United States, "the majority rules," we say truly. But the majority has no more right to rule unjustly, than has an autocratic monarchy. *The majority has a right to do what it pleases only when it pleases to do what is right!* A mere majority vote cannot make injustice just! It cannot make a wrong deed right! And the Constitution protects you in your rights when you are in the minority—even when you are a minority of one!

## Our Covenanted Rights

Read carefully the first ten Amendments to the Constitution,—often called our "Bill of Rights"—which were declared in force on Dec. 15, 1791. See how carefully they *guarantee to you and to every other citizen* of the United States, *precisely those personal rights,* that *protection by law,* which is lacking in Russia, and which makes life worth living where good government prevails. The Constitution is your safeguard. In Russia, for lack of a constitution, accepted and obeyed, soviet rule permits houses to be entered, ransacked and gutted, under pretense of authorized right of search (see Art. IV, Amendments to the Constitution, p. 38); men and women to be arrested, imprisoned indefinitely, or executed without trial (see Amendments, Arts. V, VI, VII and VIII, pp. 38,39); no property rights are respected; crops cannot be raised; factories are taken from their owners under the pretense of using them for the common profit, but are ruined and cease to operate.

The existence of free governments, with those "covenanted securities" which they afford to liberty, is no happy accident. No one object which men have proposed to themselves has called for such long-continued, strenuous, yet ennobling and beneficent effort as has the establishment of liberty in institutions and laws, such as protect us under our Constitution. Let not us who are "to the manner born," undervalue our birthright. Too seldom do we recall the cost to earlier generations of the contests which have made possible such a government as ours. We forget the long-continued, life-consuming struggle by which there has been won and established for us that constitutional liberty which is the proudest heirloom of the English-speaking race.

## Battle-monuments in Legal Terms

The noblest battle-monuments in the world are to be seen in certain of the customs and the legal terms in which are fossilized the history of centuries of soul-animating struggles for the establishment and the defense of human rights by law and in political institutions.

*"Trial by a jury of one's peers."* What an enormous advance in the conception of the worth of the average man in chronicles! What obstinate and determined struggles to keep this the law of the land, so that not the weight of the sword or of the long purse, not the will of the privileged nobles, or the subtle policy of a worldly church with its far-reaching temporal ambitions, should be allowed to decide the question of the guilt of the accused private citizen; but the facts should be found by the sound sense of twelve common men, his "peers," when they had heard the evidence, and the laws and customs of the land should then be fairly applied in every case. No wonder that a brilliant Englishman has declared that "the great end of the English Constitution is to get twelve honest men into a (jury) box!"

Or that safeguard of personal rights so dear to countless generations of our ancestors, which finds expression in the phrase, *"my house is my castle!"* Remember how that principle was wrought into law and life, and kept there through ages in which flourished plundering baron-robbers and lawless soldiers! What countless unchronicled deeds of heroism on the part of obscure and forgotten ancestors of ours, who lost all, and dared death, rather than surrender this right!—a right so precious to them and to us.

Recall the horrors of arbitrary arrest, when by *"lettres de cachet"* citizens were apprehended without pretense of trial, and mysteriously disappeared into the living sepulchres of the Bastille;—and then recall with pride and joy the long contest which preceded in England, and has always accompanied, that simple legal form, the protection of the unjustly imprisoned, in which the judge says to the officer of the law, "Do thou have his body before me, to show cause in court why he should be detained as a prisoner." Where is there a nobler battle-monument to victory won for personal liberty, than in the Latin phrase so heedlessly on our lips, the right of *"habeas corpus?"*

Generations of self-denying and public-spirited effort on the part of our ancestors have made possible for us the free, secure life we live, under a government whose fundamental law so fully "establishes justice, ensures domestic tranquillity, and promotes the general welfare."

These guaranteed rights of citizenship the American citizen by virtue of our Constitution, carries with him, wherever he may go, by land or sea. The exercise of absolute religious freedom in the choice of his form of worship; and the assured right of citizens to assemble peacefully and to petition the law-making branch of our government for such new laws, or such modifications of existing laws, as may seem desirable and needful, the Constitution guarantees to all.

## The Rules of the Game

Why does not the "rule of the majority" in the United States lead to the anarchistic violation of all rights? Because we have, and we obey, a Constitution in which the people have fixed by a great fundamental law just limitations upon the power of those who make, enforce and administer the laws. Because we are an organized state—a government where the "rules of the game" are fixed in advance, and are obeyed. The business and the great joyous game of living justly, kindly and helpfully along with other human beings, we carry on under clearly defined and universally accepted "rules of the game"—under our Constitution. Every great organic enterprise which men together undertake must have its constitution, its charter. And so must the greatest, most important business, the most engrossing and intensely interesting occupation the world knows anything about— the business of good government. To learn, and to practice well the art of being a good American citizen, one must know and must care for the Constitution—the "rules of the game"— the charter of our rights—the incorporating act of our business as a nation.

The worst enemies of our American system here in our own land are found among those who know nothing of our Constitution as a practical force in life. They are utterly ignorant of the spirit of our institutions. The firm maintenance of law and order, they think of as tyranny. Red anarchists who have lived under European tyrannies and have learned to hate absolutism in an unjust autocracy—come into our life utterly blind and deaf to the justice and the vital importance of self-government. *They knew nothing of obedience to law, voluntarily rendered, because the laws are made by the people who obey them.*

## Allegiance to Law, or Freedom Is Lost

It is only through the prevalence of the spirit of allegiance to law, that a free government like our own can continue to exist. In 1831, that brilliant young Frenchman, de Tocqueville, after two years of residence among us to study our life and the spirit of our institutions, wrote thus of what he saw: "However irksome an enactment may be, the citizen of the United States complies with it, not only because it is the work of the majority, but because it is *his own,* and he regards it as a contract to which he is himself a party." This spirit is the very essence of self-governing representative government. Obey the laws you have yourselves made! Change the laws, by the methods you have yourselves prescribed, if you believe they should be altered. But obey them while they continue to be the law of the land. This feeling of allegiance to law because it is a just law which we the people have ourselves made, is a spirit utterly unknown to the anarchists who come to the United States from foreign tyrannies. In some way, their spirit of hatred for law and order must be overcome by our spirit of willing allegiance to laws we have made, or "government deriving its just powers from the consent of the governed" will cease to have a meaning!

Yes, it will cease to exist! Could a friendly observer write of us now as de Tocqueville wrote then: "In the United States the numerous and turbulent multitude does not exist, who, regarding the law as their natural enemy look upon it with fear and distrust?" Unless the true American spirit of willing allegiance to laws we ourselves make, can be kept strong enough to penetrate and pervade the mind and life of the multitudes who have come to us from Europe and Asia, ought we not to guard our gates and check the influx of others until we have more thoroughly assimilated the mass of those who have already come?

Those anarchists and red socialists who have lived in states where tyrants made and enforced unjust laws and in governing disregarded all rights of the individual, have come to feel that anyone who loves liberty and stands for his rights, must be and should be "*against the government.*" So they are "against law"—against government—in favor of red "internationalism." They are opposed to all true love of one's own country, one's own people, and one's own government. They have never experienced the good results of self-government through the people's chosen representatives, under a constitution which the people themselves have made, to render stable their own chosen form of government. Such anarchists and "red-flag socialists"—manifestly hostile to all that we hold sacred in government, should be sent back out of our country. To all our principles they are actively hostile. There is no place for them here in America.

### Freedom of Speech and Press

The Constitution rightly provides protection for "freedom of speech and of the press." This is a right vital to the existence of an intelligent, self-governing people. We do well to guard it jealously.

But there never was a right to "freedom of speech," or of printing, which justified persons in uttering or printing "anything which they might wish to say." No one ever had a "right" to utter lies, to disseminate false reports, or to claim the protection of law and of the government while saying or printing that which advocates, defends, or directly tends to incite opposition to the reign of law and favors warfare upon established government! Nothing in history is more utterly unreasonable than is the position of the men and women who advocate violence and the destruction of all government, and yet claim that because "speech is free," the very government they are trying to destroy is under obligation to "protect" them, in their efforts by speech and publication to destroy it! They are as unreasonable in their claim as would be an assassin who was trying to kill a policeman, should he demand of the other policemen who came running to the support of law and government, that they defend the assassin in his "rights" until he had entirely murdered the officer of the law, whom he was trying to kill! Always the right to "freedom of speech" is *limited by the truth, and by due regard for facts as they are.* And no citizen and no body of citizens, no newspaper and no "correspondent," ever had a right to claim the protection of a government in the manifest attempt by him to destroy all government in general, and the government that protected him in particular. Not by mob violence should such violations of others' rights by unlicensed and untruthful speech be punished. But by due process of law it should be prevented or duly punished. There was never a "right to lie." And no government was ever bound to aid, favor, and protect in their utterance of falsehoods, those who were trying to destroy the power whose protection they invoked.

The hundreds of thousands of immigrants

who have come to be dwellers in our country and under our government we must plan to make familiar with the principles of our Constitution. Get copies of it into their hands and start sympathetic study of its provisions, its methods, and its spirit of justice and universal brotherhood, in society governed by laws which the people make and *the people mean to obey, and mean to see obeyed by all who live under the protection of our laws!*

## Why the Constitution Was Ordained

After the struggle for independence, the hardest part of the battle for national life and a workable constitution often comes after the victory by arms has been won. With us, after we had won from England by force of arms the Independence for which we made our Declaration to the world in 1776, there followed seven years after the peace of 1783 which were fraught with dangers to our young Republic even more threatening than the risks of the seven years of war which preceded them. The thirteen independent Colonies, each conscious of its own peculiar and characteristic history and institutions and inclined to be jealous of its neighbors, had won the war by co-operation under the vague authority of the Continental Congress and the Articles of Confederation. The powers of the Confederate Government thus formed were entirely inadequate to the task of setting up and maintaining a Union which could successfully govern a continent, and hold together millions of people in a state which should command the respect of the world. On February 25, 1787, James Madison wrote: "Our situation is becoming every day more and more critical. No money comes into the federal treasury; no respect is paid to the federal authority; and people of reflection unanimously agree that the existing Confederacy is tottering to its foundation." On April 8th he wrote: "I hold it for a fundamental point, that an individual independence of the states is utterly irreconcilable with the idea of an aggregate sovereignty." "Let it be tried, then, whether any middle ground can be taken, which will at once support a due supremacy of the national authority, and leave in force the local authorities so far as they can be subordinately useful."

In opening the main business in the Constitutional Convention called to form a more perfect union, and assembled in 1787, four years after peace was declared, Edmund Randolph proceeded to enumerate the defects of the old Confederation. (See the "Debates" in the "Madison Papers.")

He said: "The Confederation produced no security against foreign invasion, Congress not being permitted to prevent war, nor to support it by its own authority." "Congress could not cause infraction of treaties, nor of the law of nations, to be punished; particularly states might, by their conduct, provoke war without control." "The Federal government could not check the quarrels between states, nor a rebellion, in any, not having constitutional power or means to interpose, according to the exigency." The Federal government could not defend itself against encroachments from the states. "It was not even paramount to the state constitutions, ratified as it was in many of the states."

## "We, the People of the United States"

Let us always bear in mind the fact that the *Government of the United States is a National Government,* and rests upon a Constitution which *derives its authority from the people of the United States,* and not from the governments of the thirteen Colonies which rebelled against England, and at first claimed recognition and authority as thirteen independent sovereign states. For a few years, these thirteen independent sovereignties were acting merely as a

Confederation. But the people, under our system the ultimate sovereign power of the United States, through the work of the Convention to frame a Constitution, and the ratification of that Constitution by the people, distinctly declared, "We, the people of the United States, * * * do ordain and establish this Constitution for the United States of America."

## The Nation and the States

Article VI, Sec. 2, of the Constitution, provides that "this Constitution, and the laws of the United States which shall be made in pursuance thereof; and all treaties made, or which shall be made, under the authority of the United States, shall be the supreme law of the land; and the judges in every state shall be bound thereby, anything in the constitution or laws of any state to the contrary notwithstanding."

Doubly to insure this supreme authority of the Federal Constitution and the Federal laws, it is provided in a following section (Art. VI, Sec. 3) that "The Senators and Representatives before mentioned, and the members of the several state legislatures, and all executive and judicial officers, both of the United States and of the several states, shall be bound, by oath or affirmation, to support this Constitution."

## Read, Mark, and Learn

Our Constitution is the very heart and life of the nation we love. Other nations the world over have copied it. Evidently, our fathers expected the people of the United States to be familiar with the Constitution in all its essential provisions. Yet there have been thousands of office-holders, under the Federal government and the forty-eight state governments of the Union, who have sworn to support the Constitution, yet have never once read it through! In an average audience of a thousand Americans, how many will you find who have a copy of the Constitution within reach? How many who have "never read it"? Every good American ought to have a copy of it for his own use, easily accessible for reference.

When foreigners wish to become American citizens, the judge who examines them for their naturalization papers is required to have good evidence that the applicant is "attached to the principles of our government." How many of the principles of our government could you state clearly?

There is a great revival of interest in the Constitution, in these last few years. Now that hundreds and thousands of women are preparing to vote intelligently, while tens of thousands of Boy Scouts and Camp Fire Girls are informing themselves upon questions of government, it is coming to be regarded as more and more manifestly the duty of every man and woman, to know the essential provisions of our Constitution.

## The Constitution and the Workingman

Especially should every workingman and woman become familiar with the Constitution. It is the workingman's best friend. It not only protects him in his personal freedom and his political rights, it assures to him the full and regular payment of the wages he contracts to work for. It protects his savings. It guards his home. It respects and protects his family life. Courts and the judges by some of whose decisions he sometimes has felt himself aggrieved, are nevertheless the workingman's best friends. It is by the keen sense of justice and the trained intelligence of our judges, that the workingman is protected against the ruinous effects of misguided attempts at legislation which would (if it could) set aside or overthrow the safeguards with which our fundamental law has surrounded us. It is the careful and just administration of our government, guarded and insured by our courts, that keeps our national life secure.

## The Constitution and the Courts

The power intrusted by the Constitution to our Supreme Court, to pass judgment upon the constitutionality of any state or federal law which in a definite case involving the application of the law, is duly brought before the court, and to declare unconstitutional any provisions in such a law which would ignore or violate any provision of the Constitution—is the crowning glory of our American system. This has been and still is the surest safeguard for the liberties and the rights of each one of us, citizens of the United States. The Constitution lays down the essential principles and prescribes the form and functions of our government. It is, as it should be, comparatively brief. It deals only with essential provisions which are universally applicable throughout the extent of the nation and for long periods of time. It is not meant to be easily altered. The Constitution is created and adopted by the people, and is the supreme conditioning law of our national state. The manifold enactments of Congress and of the state legislatures in their sphere, are valid only when they conform to the Constitution—our Supreme National Law. Of course it is essential to our system that we have a Supreme Court to decide whether enactments of these various lawmaking bodies are in harmony with the principles and the provisions of the Constitution.

Study the Constitution. See how the law and the courts protect you. Let no demagogue persuade you to advocate changes which would make it impossible for our courts to have strong and fearless judges to continue to defend us in our constitutional rights. That any man who has succeeded in securing an election to the Senate of the United States could so utterly fail to understand the essential spirit of the Constitution he has sworn to support, as to be capable of proposing a law to impeach and remove any judge who should pronounce a bill passed by Congress "unconstitutional," is one of the wonders of American politics!

## The Glory and the Responsibility of Citizenship

It is no small thing to be a citizen of the world's greatest Republic! It is a great responsibility to be a voter here. You want to know your privileges and your power as an American voter; and you want to know your duties and responsibilities, as well as your rights, under the Constitution. Think them out, for yourself, as you read and study the clear provisions of our great fundamental law. We cannot all be learned constitutional lawyers. But every American citizen, man or woman, young or old, may have and should have an intelligent idea of our form of representative government "of the people, by the people, for the people." Every one of us should know and should value the security it guarantees to each of us in guarding for us our enjoyment of "life, liberty, and the pursuit of happiness."

Let each one of us have a copy of our title-deed to our rights as American citizens. Let us read, think about, and discuss with our friends, the Constitution which is the charter of our National Life. Study its principles. Know it! Then we shall love it! Do not fancy that you can play well the great game of American life, without knowing the Rules of the Game! One flag, one country, one nation! Let us love our own country, honor our own flag! Not for us the red flag of a false and anarchistic internationalism; but the Red, White and Blue for which our fathers and brothers and sons have died; under which, please God, we will live, and for which if need be we will die—faithful to the brotherhood of the whole human race, by being first of all faithful to our own home, our own family, our own community, and to the land we love!

Let us live, as the inscription on the monument to the Three Hundred Spartans at Thermopylae says they died. They willingly, valiantly, and with the most fearless and confident alacrity, gave up their lives in the narrow pass, three hundred of them, to hold back the tens of thousand of Asiatics who were threatening to overwhelm the liberty and civilization of Europe. Many of our sons and brothers have in these last two years died willingly in a like struggle to defend liberty and the reign of law against tyranny and brute force. The epitaph on the monument of the deathless Three Hundred who made the stand at Thermopylae which saved their native land, all Europe, and our own Western civilization, was these words: "Stranger, go tell the Lacedomonians that we lie here, *obedient to their laws!*"

So let us live for Freedom and Good Government—willingly "obedient to our laws."

# Biography of Merrill Edward Gates, 1848-1922

Born April 6, 1848, Merrill Edward Gates distinguished himself during the 74 years he lived as a scholar and educator, administrator, lecturer, author, government official, and churchman.

He earned a Ph.D. at New York State University in 1889, received an LH.D. from Columbia University in 1887 and was further honored with LL.D. degrees from Princeton University (1882), Rochester University (1882), Columbia University (1891) and Williams College (1893).

Dr. Gates served two institutions of higher learning as president: Rutgers University (1882-1890) and Amherst College (1890-1899).

In addition to a career as educator and academic administrator, Dr. Gates was a member, chairman and secretary of the U.S. Board of Indian Commissioners, became a licensed preacher of the Congregational Church in 1899, served as vice president of both the American Bible Society and the American Tract Society and as president of the American Missionary Association (1892-1898). For 20 years he was also a member of the International Commission of the YMCA.

Dr. Gates was the author of *International Arbitration* (1897) and *Highest Use of Wealth* (1901).

His son, Seth M. Gates, was a congressman.

Merrill Edward Gates died August 11, 1922.

# Objects for Which The Constitution Was Established

## ARTICLE I.

### The Legislative Power.

Section 1. The Congress of the United States.

Section 2. The House of Representatives.

Section 3. The Senate.

Section 4. Election of Senators and Representatives—Meetings of Congress.

Section 5. Powers and Duties of Each House—Journals—Adjournments.

Section 6. Compensation of Senators and Representatives—Privilege from Arrest—Freedom of Speech and Debate—Holding Other Offices.

Section 7. Process of Legislation—President's Veto Power.

Section 8. Enumerated Powers of Congress.

Section 9. Prohibitions and Limitations on Powers of Congress.

Section 10. Restrictions on Powers of the States.

## ARTICLE II.

### The Executive Power.

Section 1. The President—Term of Office—Election—Qualifications—Succession of Vice President—Compensation—Oath of Office.

Section 2. Enumerated Powers and Duties of President.

Section 3. Relations of President with Congress—Diplomatic Business—Execution of the Laws.

Section 4. Impeachment of President and Other Officers.

## ARTICLE III.

### The Judicial Power.

Section 1. Supreme Court of the United States and Other Federal Courts—Tenure of Judges—Compensation.

Section 2. Jurisdiction of United States Courts—Original and Appellate Jurisdiction of Supreme Court—Trial by Jury—Place of Trial.

Section 3. Treason against the United States—Definition and Punishment.

## ARTICLE IV.

### Interstate Relations.

Section 1. Full Faith and Credit to Public Arts, Records, and Proceedings.

Section 2. Interstate Privileges and Immunities of Citizenship—Extradition—Fugitive Slaves.

Section 3. Admission and Formation of New States—Public Lands.

Section 4. Guaranty of Republican Government—Protection of States against Invasion and Domestic Violence.

## ARTICLE V.

*Amendment of the Constitution.*

Proposal of Amendments by Congress—Convention for Proposing Amendments—Ratification of Amendments

## ARTICLE VI.

*Miscellaneous Provisions.*

Validity of the Public Debt—The Constitution the Supreme Law of the Land—Oath of Public Officers to Support the Constitution—No Religious Test Required.

## ARTICLE VII.

Ratification and Establishment of the Constitution.

# Constitution of the United States

## Preamble to the Constitution of the United States

We the People of the United States, in Order to form a more perfect Union, establish Justice, insure domestic Tranquility, provide for the common defence, promote the general Welfare, and secure the Blessings of Liberty to ourselves and our Posterity, do ordain and establish this Constitution for the United States of America.

### ARTICLE I.

**Section 1.** All legislative Powers herein granted shall be vested in a Congress of the United States, which shall consist of a Senate and House of Representatives.

**Section 2.** The House of Representatives shall be composed of Members chosen every second Year by the People of the Several States, and the Electors in each State shall have the Qualifications requisite for Electors of the most numerous Branch of the State Legislature.

No Person shall be a Representative who shall not have attained to the Age of twenty-five Years, and been seven Years a Citizen of the United States, and who shall not, when elected, be an Inhabitant of that State in which he shall be chosen.

*[Representatives and direct Taxes shall be apportioned among the several States which may be included within this Union, according to their respective Numbers, which shall be determined by adding to the whole Number of free Persons, including those bound to Service for a Term of Years, and excluding Indians not taxed, three fifths of all other Persons.] The actual Enumeration shall be made within three Years

after the first Meeting of the Congress of the United States, and within every subsequent Term of ten Years, in such Manner as they shall by Law direct. The Number of Representatives shall not exceed one for every thirty Thousand, but each State shall have at Least one Representative; and until such enumeration shall be made, the State of New Hampshire shall be entitled to choose three, Massachusetts eight, Rhode Island and Providence Plantations one, Connecticut five, New York six; New Jersey four, Pennsylvania eight, Delaware one, Maryland six, Virginia ten, North Carolina five, South Carolina five, and Georgia three.

---

*The clause included in brackets is amended by the 14th amendment, 2d section.

When vacancies happen in the Representation from any State, the Executive Authority thereof shall issue Writs of Election to fill such Vacancies.

The House of Representatives shall choose their Speaker and other Officers; and shall have the sole Power of Impeachment.

**Section 3.** The Senate, of the United States shall be composed of two Senators from each State, chosen by the Legislature thereof, for six Years; and each Senator shall have one Vote.

Immediately after they shall be assembled in Consequence of the first Election, they shall be divided as equally as may be into three Classes. The Seats of the Senators of the first Class shall be vacated at the Expiration of the second year, of the second Class at the Expiration of the fourth Year, and of the third Class at the Expiration of the sixth Year, so that one-third may be chosen every second year; and if Vacancies happen by Resignation, or otherwise, during the Recess of the Legislature of any State, the Executive thereof may make temporary Appointments until the next Meeting of the Legislature, which shall then fill such Vacancies.

No Person shall be a Senator who shall not have attained to the Age of thirty Years, and been nine Years a Citizen of the United States, and who shall not, when elected, be an Inhabitant of that State for which he shall be chosen.

The Vice President of the United States shall be President of the Senate, but shall have no Vote, unless they be equally divided.

The Senate shall choose their other Officers, and also a President pro tempore, in the Absence of the Vice President, or when he shall exercise the Office of President of the United States.

The Senate shall have the sole Power to try all Impeachments. When sitting for that Purpose, they shall be on Oath or Affirmation. When the President of the United States is tried, the Chief Justice shall preside: And no Person shall be convicted without the Concurrence of two thirds of the Members present.

Judgment in Cases of Impeachment shall not extend further than to removal from Office, and disqualification to hold and enjoy any Office of honor, Trust or Profit under the United States: but the Party convicted shall nevertheless be liable and subject to Indictment, Trial, Judgment and Punishment, according to Law.

**Section 4.** The Times, Places and Manner of holding Elections for Senators and Representatives, shall be prescribed in each State by the Legislature thereof; but the Congress may at any time by Law make or alter such Regulations, except as to the Places of choosing Senators.

The Congress shall assemble at least once in every Year, and such Meeting shall be on the first Monday in December, unless they shall by Law appoint a different Day.

**Section 5.** Each House shall be the Judge of the Elections, Returns and Qualifications of its own Members, and a Majority of each shall constitute a Quorum to do Business; but a smaller Number may adjourn from day to day, and may be authorized to compel the Attendance of absent Members, in such Manner, and under such Penalties as each House may provide.

Each House may determine the Rules of its Proceedings, punish its Members for disorderly Behavior, and, with the Concurrence of two thirds, expel a Member.

Each House shall keep a Journal of its Proceedings, and from time to time publish the same, excepting such Parts as may in their Judgment require Secrecy; and the Yeas and Nays of the Members of either House on any question shall, at the Desire of one fifth of those present, be entered on the Journal.

Neither House, during the Session of Congress, shall, without the Consent of the other, adjourn for more than three days, nor to any other Place than that in which the two Houses shall be sitting.

**Section 6.** The Senators and Representatives shall receive a Compensation for their Services, to be ascertained by Law, and paid out of the Treasury of the United States. They shall in all Cases, except Treason, Felony and Breach of the Peace, be privileged from Arrest during their Attendance at the Session of their respective Houses, and in going to and returning from the same; and for any Speech or Debate in either House, they shall not be questioned in any other Place.

No Senator or Representative shall, during the Time for which he was elected, be appointed to any civil Office under the Authority of the United States, which shall have been created, or the Emoluments whereof shall have been increased during such time; and no Person holding any Office under the United States, shall be a Member of either House during his Continuance in Office.

**Section 7.** All Bills for raising Revenue shall originate in the House of Representatives; but the Senate may propose or concur with Amendments as on other Bills.

Every Bill which shall have passed the House of Representatives and the Senate, shall, before it becomes a Law, be presented to the President of the United States; If he approve he shall sign it, but if not he shall return it, with his Objections to that House in which it shall have originated, who shall enter the Objections at large on their Journal, and proceed to reconsider it. If after such Reconsideration two thirds of that House shall agree to pass the Bill, it shall be sent, together with the Objections, to the other House, by which it shall likewise be reconsidered, and if approved by two thirds of that House, it shall become a Law. But in all such Cases the Votes of both Houses shall be determined by Yeas and Nays, and the Names of the Persons voting for and against the Bill shall be entered on the Journal of each House respectively. If any Bill shall not be returned by the President within ten Days (Sundays excepted) after it shall have been presented to him, the Same shall be a Law, in like Manner as if he had signed it, unless the Congress by their Adjournment prevent its Return, in which Case it shall not be a Law.

Every Order, Resolution, or Vote to which the Concurrence of the Senate and House of Representatives may be necessary (except on a question of Adjournment) shall be presented to the President of the United States; and before the Same shall take Effect, shall be approved by him, or being disapproved by him, shall be repassed by two thirds of the Senate and House of Representatives, according to the Rules and Limitations prescribed in the Case of a Bill.

**Section 8.** The Congress shall have Power To lay and collect Taxes, Duties, Imposts and Excises, to pay the Debts and provide for the common Defense and general Welfare of the United States; but all Duties, Imposts and Excises shall be uniform throughout the United States;

To borrow Money on the credit of the United States;

To regulate Commerce with foreign Nations, and among the several States, and with the Indian Tribes;

To establish an uniform Rule of Naturalization, and uniform Laws on the subject of Bankruptcies throughout the United States;

To coin Money, regulate the Value thereof, and of foreign Coin, and fix the Standard of Weights and Measures;

To provide for the Punishment of counterfeiting the Securities and current Coin of the United States;

To establish Post Offices and post Roads;

To promote the Progress of Science and useful Arts, by securing for limited Times to Authors and Inventors the exclusive Rights to their respective Writings and Discoveries;

To constitute Tribunals inferior to the supreme Court;

To define and punish Piracies and Felonies committed on the high Seas, and Offences against the Law of Nations;

To declare War, grant Letters of Marque and Reprisal, and make Rules concerning Captures on Land and Water;

To raise and support Armies, but no Appropriation of Money to that Use shall be for a longer Term than two Years;

To provide and maintain a Navy;

To make Rules for the Government and Regulation of the land and naval Forces;

To provide for calling forth the Militia to execute the Laws of the Union, suppress Insurrections and repel Invasions;

To provide for organizing, arming, and disciplining, the Militia, and for governing such Part of them as may be employed in the Service of the United States, reserving to the States respectively, the Appointment of the Officers, and the Authority of training the Militia according to the discipline prescribed by Congress;

To exercise exclusive Legislation in all Cases whatsoever, over such District (not exceeding ten Miles square) as may, by Cession of particular States, and the Acceptance of Congress, become the Seat of the Government of the United States, and to exercise like Authority over all Places purchased by the Consent of the Legislature of the State in which the Same shall be, for the Erection of Forts, Magazines, Arsenals, dock-Yards, and other needful Buildings;—And

To make all Laws which shall be necessary and proper for carrying into Execution the foregoing Powers, and all other Powers vested by this Constitution in the Government of the United States, or in any Department or Officer thereof.

**Section 9.** The Migration or Importation of such Persons as any of the States now existing shall think proper to admit, shall not be prohibited by the Congress prior to the Year one thousand eight hundred and eight, but a Tax or duty may be imposed on such Importation, not exceeding ten dollars for each Person.

The Privilege of the Writ of Habeas Corpus shall not be suspended, unless when in Cases of Rebellion or Invasion the public Safety may require it.

No Bill of Attainder or expost facto Law shall be passed.

No Capitation, or other direct, tax shall be laid, unless in Proportion to the Census or Enumeration herein before directed to be taken.

No Tax or Duty shall be laid on Articles exported from any State.

No preference shall be given by any Regulation of Commerce or Revenue to the Ports of one State over those of another: nor shall Vessels bound to, or from, one State, be obliged to enter, clear, or pay Duties in another.

No Money shall be drawn from the Treasury, but in Consequence of Appropriations made by Law; and a regular Statement and Account of the Receipts and Expenditures of all public Money shall be published from time to time.

No Title of Nobility shall be granted by the United States: And no Person holding any Office of Profit or Trust under them, shall, without the Consent of the Congress, accept of any present, Emolument, Office, or Title, of any kind whatever, from any King, Prince, or foreign State.

**Section 10.** No State shall enter into any Treaty, Alliance, or Confederation; grant Letters of Marque and Reprisal; coin Money, emit Bills of Credit; make any Thing but gold and silver Coin a Tender in Payment of Debts; pass any Bill of Attainder, ex post facto Law, or Law impairing the Obligation of Contracts, or grant any Title of Nobility.

No State shall, without the Consent of the Congress, lay any Imposts or Duties on Imports or Exports, except what may be absolutely necessary for executing its inspection Laws: and the net Produce of all Duties and Imposts, laid by any State on Imports or Exports, shall be for the Use of the Treasury of the United States; and all such Laws shall be subject to the Revision and Control of the Congress.

No State shall, without the Consent of Congress, lay any Duty of Tonnage, keep Troops, or Ships of War in time of Peace, enter into any Agreement or Compact with another State, or with a foreign Power, or engage in War, unless actually invaded, or in such imminent Danger as will not admit of delay.

# ARTICLE II.

**Section 1.** The executive Power shall be vested in a President of the United States of America. He shall hold his Office during the Term of four Years, and, together with the Vice President, chosen for the same Term, be elected, as follows

Each State shall appoint in such Manner as the Legislature thereof may direct, a Number of Electors, equal to the whole Number of Senators and Representatives to which the State may be entitled in the Congress: but no Senator or Representative, or Person holding an Office of Trust or Profit under the United States, shall be appointed an Elector.

["The electors shall meet in their respective States, and vote by ballot for two Persons, of whom one at least shall not be an Inhabitant of the same State with themselves. And they shall make a list of all the Persons voted for, and of the Number of Votes for each; which List they shall sign and certify, and transmit sealed to the Seat of the Government of the United States, directed to the President of the Senate. The President of the Senate shall, in the Presence of the Senate and House of Representatives, open all the Certificates, and the Votes shall then be counted. The Person having the greatest Number of Votes shall be the President, if such Number be a Majority of the whole Number of Electors appointed; and if there be more than one who have such Majority, and have an equal Number of Votes, then the House of Representatives shall immediately choose by Ballot one of them for President; and if no Person have a Majority, then from the five highest on the List the said House shall in like Manner choose the President. But in choosing the President, the Votes shall be taken by States, the Representation from each State having one Vote; A quorum for this Purpose shall consist of a Member or Members from two-thirds of the

States, and a Majority of all the States shall be necessary to a Choice. In every Case, after the Choice of the President, the Person having the greatest Number of Votes of the Electors shall be the Vice President. But if there should remain two or more who have equal votes, the Senate shall choose from them by Ballot the Vice-President."]

(This clause has been superseded by the twelfth amendment, p. 39.)

The Congress may determine the Time of choosing the Electors, and the Day on which they shall give their Votes; which Day shall be the same throughout the United States.

No Person except a natural born Citizen, or a Citizen of the United States, at the time of the Adoption of this Constitution, shall be eligible to the Office of President; neither shall any Person be eligible to that Office who shall not have attained to the age of thirty-five Years, and been fourteen Years a Resident within the United States.

In Case of the Removal of the President from Office, or of his Death, Resignation, or Inability to discharge the Powers and Duties of the said Office, the same shall devolve on the Vice President, and the Congress may by Law provide for the Case of Removal, Death, Resignation, or Inability, both of the President and Vice President, declaring what Officer shall then act as President, and such Officer shall act accordingly, until the Disability be removed, or a President shall be elected.

The President shall, at stated Times, receive for his Services, a Compensation, which shall neither be increased nor diminished during the Period for which he shall have been elected, and he shall not receive within that Period any other Emolument from the United States, or any of them.

Before he enter on the Execution of his Office, he shall take the following Oath or Affirmation:—"I do solemnly swear (or affirm) that I will faithfully execute the Office of President of the United States, and will to the best of my Ability, preserve, protect and defend the Constitution of the United States."

**Section 2.** The President shall be Commander in Chief of the Army and Navy of the United States, and of the Militia of the several States, when called into the actual Service of the United States; he may require the Opinion, in writing, of the principal Officer in each of the executive Departments, upon any Subject relating to the Duties of their respective Offices, and he shall have Power to grant Reprieves and Pardons for Offenses against the United States, except in Cases of Impeachment.

He shall have Power, by and with the Advice and Consent of the Senate, to make Treaties, provided two thirds of the Senators present concur; and he shall nominate, and by and with the Advice and Consent of the Senate, shall appoint Ambassadors, other public Ministers and Consuls, Judges of the supreme Court, and all other Officers of the United States, whose Appointments are not herein otherwise provided for, and which shall be established by Law: but the Congress may by Law vest the Appointment of such inferior Officers, as they think proper, in the President alone, in the Courts of Law, or in the Heads of Departments.

The President shall have Power to fill up all Vacancies that may happen during the Recess of the Senate, by granting Commissions which shall expire at the End of their next Session.

**Section 3.** He shall from time to time give to the Congress Information of the State of the Union, and recommend to their Consideration such Measures as he shall judge necessary and expedient; he may, on extraordinary Occasions, convene both Houses, or either of them, and in Case of Disagreement between them, with Respect to the Time of Adjournment, he may adjourn them to such Time as he shall think proper; he shall receive Ambassadors and other public Ministers; he shall take Care that the Laws be faithfully executed, and shall Commission all the Officers of the United States.

**Section 4.** The President, Vice President and all civil Officers of the United States, shall be removed from Office on Impeachment for, and Conviction of, Treason, Bribery, or other high Crimes and Misdemeanors.

### ARTICLE III.

**Section 1.** The judicial Power of the United States, shall be vested in one supreme Court, and in such inferior Courts as the Congress may from time to time ordain and establish. The Judges, both of the supreme and inferior Courts, shall hold their Offices during good Behaviour, and shall, at stated Times, receive for their Services, a Compensation, which shall not be diminished during their Continuance in Office.

**Section 2.** The judicial Power shall extend to all Cases, in Law and Equity, arising under this Constitution, the Laws of the United States, and Treaties made, or which shall be made, under their Authority:—to all Cases affecting Ambassadors, other public Ministers and Consuls;—to all Cases of admiralty and maritime Jurisdiction;—to Controversies to which the United States shall be a Party;—to Controversies between two or more States;—between a State and Citizens of another State;—between Citizens of different States,—between Citizens of the same State claiming Lands under Grants of different States, and between a State, or the Citizens thereof, and foreign States, Citizens or Subjects.

In all Cases affecting Ambassadors, other public Ministers and Consuls, and those in which a State shall be Party, the supreme Court shall have original Jurisdiction. In all the other Cases before mentioned, the supreme Court shall have appellate Jurisdiction, both as to Law and Fact, with such Exceptions, and under such Regulations as the Congress shall make.

The Trial of all Crimes, except in Cases of Impeachment, shall be by Jury; and such Trial shall be held in the State where the said Crimes shall have been committed; but when not committed within any State, the Trial shall be at such Place or Places as the Congress may by Law have directed.

**Section 3.** Treason against the United States, shall consist only in levying War against them, or in adhering to their Enemies, giving them Aid and Comfort. No Person shall be convicted of Treason unless on the Testimony of two Witnesses to the same overt Act, or on Confession in open Court.

The Congress shall have Power to declare the Punishment of Treason, but no Attainder of Treason shall work Corruption of Blood, or Forfeiture except during the Life of the Person attainted.

### ARTICLE IV.

**Section 1.** Full Faith and Credit shall be given in each State to the public Acts, Records, and judicial Proceedings of every other State. And the Congress may by general Laws prescribe the Manner in which such Acts, Records and Proceedings shall be proved, and the Effect thereof.

**Section 2.** The Citizens of each State shall be entitled to all Privileges and Immunities of Citizens in the several States.

A person charged in any State with Treason, Felony, or other Crime, who shall flee from Justice, and be found in another State, shall on Demand of the executive Authority of the State from which he fled, be delivered up to be removed to the State having Jurisdiction of the Crime.

No Person held to Service or Labour in one State, under the Laws thereof, escaping into another, shall, in Consequence of any Law or Regulation therein, be discharged from such Service or Labour, but shall be delivered up on Claim of the Party to whom such Service or Labour may be due.

**Section 3.** New States may be admitted by the Congress into this Union; but no new State shall be formed or erected within the Jurisdiction of any other State; nor any State be formed by the Junction of two or more States, or Parts of States, without the Consent of the Legislatures of the States concerned as well as of the Congress.

The Congress shall have Power to dispose of and make all needful Rules and Regulations respecting the Territory or other Property belonging to the United States; and nothing in this Constitution shall be so construed as to Prejudice any Claims of the United States, or of any particular State.

**Section 4.** The United States shall guarantee to every State in this Union a Republican Form of Government, and shall protect each of them against Invasion; and on Application of the Legislature, or of the Executive (when the Legislature cannot be convened) against domestic Violence.

## ARTICLE V.

The Congress, whenever two thirds of both Houses shall deem it necessary, shall propose Amendments to this Constitution, or, on the Application of the Legislatures of two thirds of the several States, shall call a Convention for proposing Amendments, which, in either Case, shall be valid to all Intents and Purposes, as Part of this Constitution, when ratified by the Legislatures of three fourths of the several States, or by Conventions in three fourths thereof, as the one or the other Mode of Ratification may be proposed by the Congress; Provided that no Amendment which may be made prior to the Year One thousand eight hundred and eight shall in any Manner affect the first and fourth Clauses in the Ninth Section of the first Article; and that no State, without its Consent, shall be deprived of its equal Suffrage in the Senate.

## ARTICLE VI.

All Debts contracted and Engagements entered into, before the Adoption of this Constitution, shall be as valid against the United States under this Constitution, as under the Confederation.

This Constitution, and the Laws of the United States which shall be made in Pursuance thereof; and all Treaties made, or which shall be made, under the Authority of the United States, shall be the supreme Law of the Land; and the Judges in every State shall be bound thereby, any Thing in the Constitution or Laws of any State to the Contrary notwithstanding.

The Senators and Representatives before mentioned, and the Members of the several State Legislatures, and all executive and judicial Officers, both of the United States and of the several States, shall be bound by Oath or Affirmation, to support this Constitution; but no religious Test shall ever be required as a Qualification to any Office or public Trust under the United States.

## ARTICLE VII.

The Ratification of the Conventions of nine States, shall be sufficient for the Establishment

of this Constitution between the States so rati-
fying the Same.

DONE in Convention by the Unanimous Consent
of the States present the Seventeenth Day of
September in The Year of our Lord one thousand seven hundred and Eighty seven, and of
the Independence of the United States of
America the Twelfth.

# Amendments to the Constitution

I. Religious Freedom—Freedom of Speech and Press—Right of Assembly and Petition.

II. The Militia—Right to Keep and Bear Arms.

III. Quartering of Soldiers.

IV. Security Against Unreasonable Searches and Seizures—Search Warrants.

V. Right to Indictment by Grand Jury—Twice in Jeopardy—Privilege against Self-Crimination—Protection of Life, Liberty, and Property by Due Process of Law—Taking Private Property for Public Use.

VI. Rights of Accused in Criminal Trials.

VII. Trial by Jury in Civil Cases.

VIII. Prohibition of Excessive Bail or Fines, and Cruel and Unusual Punishments.

IX. Reservation of Rights of the People.

X. Powers Not Delegated are Reserved to the States or the People.

XI. Exemption of States from Suits by Citizens.

XII. Manner of Electing President and Vice President.

XIII. Abolition of Slavery and Involuntary Servitude.

XIV. Definition of United States Citizenship—Privileges and Immunities of Citizens not to be Abridged by States—Guaranty of Due Process of Law—Equal Protection of the Laws—Apportionment of Representatives of Congress—Disqualification for Office by Insurrection or Rebellion—Removal of Disabilities—Validity of the Public Debt.

XV. Right of Suffrage not to be denied on Account of Race, Color, or Previous Servitude.

XVI. Levy of Income Tax Without Apportionment.

XVII. Popular Election of Senators.

XVIII. National Prohibition.

XIX. Suffrage for women.

XX. Terms of President and Vice President to Begin on January 20; Those of Senators, Representatives, January 3.

XXI. Repeal of Article XVIII.

XXII. Limiting Presidential Terms of Office.

XXIII. Presidential Vote for District of Columbia.

XXIV. Barring Poll Tax in Federal Elections.

XXV. Presidential Disability and Succession.

XXVI. Lowering Voting Age to 18 Years.

ARTICLES IN ADDITION TO, AND AMENDMENT OF, THE CONSTITUTION OF THE UNITED STATES OF AMERICA, PROPOSED BY CONGRESS, AND RATIFIED BY THE LEGISLATURES OF THE SEVERAL STATES PURSUANT TO THE FIFTH ARTICLE OF THE ORIGINAL CONSTITUTION.

## [ARTICLE I.]

(First ten amendments adopted June 15, 1790)

Congress shall make no law respecting an establishment of religion, or prohibiting the free exercise thereof; or abridging the freedom of speech, or of the press; or the right of the people peaceably to assemble, and to petition the Government for a redress of grievances.

## [ARTICLE II.]

A well regulated Militia, being necessary to the security of a free State, the right of the people to keep and bear Arms, shall not be infringed.

## [ARTICLE III.]

No Soldier shall, in time of peace be quartered in any house, without the consent of the Owner, nor in time of war, but in a manner to be prescribed by law.

## [ARTICLE IV.]

The right of the people to be secure in their persons, houses, papers, and effects, against unreasonable searches and seizures, shall not be violated, and no Warrants shall issue, but upon probable cause, supported by Oath or affirmation, and particularly describing the place to be searched, and the persons or things to be seized.

## [ARTICLE V.]

No person shall be held to answer for a capital, or otherwise infamous crime, unless on a presentment or indictment of a Grand Jury, except in cases arising in the land or naval forces, or in the Militia, when in actual service in time of War or public danger; nor shall any person be subject for the same offence to be twice put in jeopardy of life or limb; nor shall be compelled in any Criminal Case to be a witness against himself, nor be deprived of life, liberty, or property, without due process of law; nor shall private property be taken for public use, without just compensation.

## [ARTICLE VI.]

In all criminal prosecutions, the accused shall enjoy the right to a speedy and public trial, by an impartial jury of the State and district wherein the crime shall have been committed, which district shall have been previously ascertained by law, and to be informed of the nature and cause of the accusation; to be confronted with the witnesses against him; to have compulsory process for obtaining Witnesses in his favor, and to have the Assistance of Counsel for his defence.

## [ARTICLE VII.]

In suits at common law, where the value in controversy shall exceed twenty dollars, the right of trial by jury shall be preserved, and no fact tried by a jury shall be otherwise re-examined in any Court of the United States, than according to the rules of the common law.

## [ARTICLE VIII.]

Excessive bail shall not be required, nor excessive fines imposed, nor cruel and unusual punishments inflicted.

## [ARTICLE IX.]

The enumeration in the Constitution, of certain rights, shall not be construed to deny or disparage others retained by the people.

## [ARTICLE X.]

The powers not delegated to the United States by the Constitution, nor prohibited by it to the

States, are reserved to the States respectively, or to the people.

## [ARTICLE XI.]

### (Adopted January 8, 1798)

The Judicial power of the United States shall not be construed to extend to any suit in law or equity, commenced or prosecuted against one of the United States by Citizens of another State, or by Citizens or Subjects of any Foreign State.

## [ARTICLE XII.]

### (Adopted September 25, 1804)

The Electors shall meet in their respective states, and vote by ballot for President and Vice-President, one of whom, at least, shall not be an inhabitant of the same state with themselves; they shall name in their ballots the person voted for as President, and in distinct ballots the person voted for as Vice-President, and they shall make distinct lists of all persons voted for as President, and of all persons voted for as Vice-President, and of the number of votes for each, which lists they shall sign and certify, and transmit sealed to the seat of the government of the United States, directed to the President of the Senate; — The President of the Senate shall, in the presence of the Senate and House of Representatives, open all the certificates and the votes shall then be counted; — The person having the greatest number of votes for President, shall be the President, if such number be a majority of the whole number of Electors appointed; and if no person have such majority, then from the persons having the highest numbers not exceeding three on the list of those voted for as President, the House of Representatives shall choose immediately, by ballot, the President. But in choosing the President, the votes shall be taken by states, the representation from each state having one vote; a quorum for this purpose shall consist of a member or members from two-thirds of the states, and a majority of all the states shall be necessary to a choice. And if the House of Representatives shall not choose a President whenever the right of choice shall devolve upon them, before the fourth day of March next following, then the Vice-President shall act as President, as in the case of the death or other constitutional disability of the President. The person having the greatest number of votes as Vice-President, shall be the Vice-President, if such number be a majority of the whole number of Electors appointed, and if no person have a majority, then from the two highest numbers on the list, the Senate shall choose the Vice-President; a quorum for the purpose shall consist of two-thirds of the whole number of Senators, and a majority of the whole number shall be necessary to a choice. But no person constitutionally ineligible to the office of President shall be eligible to that of Vice-President of the United States.

## [ARTICLE XIII.]

### (Adopted December 18, 1865)

**Section 1.** Neither slavery nor involuntary servitude, except as a punishment for crime whereof the party shall have been duly convicted, shall exist within the United States, or any place subject to their jurisdiction.

**Section 2.** Congress shall have power to enforce this article by appropriate legislation.

## [ARTICLE XIV.]

### (Adopted July 21, 1868)

**Section 1.** All persons born or naturalized in the United States, and subject to the jurisdiction thereof, are citizens of the United States and of the State wherein they reside. No State shall make or enforce any law which shall abridge the privileges or immunities of citizens of the United States; nor shall any State deprive any person of life, liberty, or property, without due process of law; nor deny to any person within its jurisdiction the equal protection of the laws.

**Section 2.** Representatives shall be apportioned among the several States according to their respective numbers, counting the whole number of persons in each State, excluding Indians not taxed. But when the right to vote at any election for the choice of electors for President and Vice President of the United States, Representatives in Congress, the Executive and Judicial officers of a State, or the members of the Legislature thereof, is denied to any of the male inhabitants of each State, being twenty-one years of age, and citizens of the United States, or in any way abridged, except for participation in rebellion, or other crime, the basis of representation therein shall be reduced in the proportion which the number of such male citizens shall bear to the whole number of male citizens twenty-one years of age in such State.

**Section 3.** No person shall be a Senator or Representative in Congress, or elector of President and Vice-President, or hold any office, civil or military, under the United States, or under any State, who, having previously taken an oath, as a member of Congress, or as an officer of the United States, or as a member of any State legislature, or as an executive or judicial officer of any State, to support the Constitution of the United States, shall have engaged in insurrection or rebellion against the same, or given aid or comfort to the enemies thereof. But Congress may by a vote of two-thirds of each House, remove such disability.

**Section 4.** The validity of the public debt of the United States, authorized by law, including debts incurred for payment of pensions and bounties for services in suppressing insurrection or rebellion, shall not be questioned. But neither the United States nor any State shall assume or pay any debt or obligation incurred in aid of insurrection or rebellion against the United States, or any claim for the loss or emancipation of any slave; but all such debts, obligations and claims shall be held illegal and void.

**Section 5.** The Congress shall have power to enforce, by appropriate legislation, the provisions of this article.

## [ARTICLE XV.]

### (Adopted March 30, 1870)

**Section 1.** The right of citizens of the United States to vote shall not be denied or abridged by the United States or by any State on account of race, color, or previous condition of servitude.

**Section 2.** The Congress shall have power to enforce this article by appropriate legislation.

## [ARTICLE XVI.]

### (Adopted February 25, 1913)

The Congress shall have power to lay and collect taxes on incomes, from whatever source derived, without apportionment among the several States, and without regard to any census or enumeration.

## [ARTICLE XVII.]

### (Adopted May 31, 1913)

The Senate of the United States shall be composed of two Senators from each State, elected by the people thereof, for six years; and each

Senator shall have one vote. The electors in each State shall have the qualifications requisite for electors of the most numerous branch of the State legislatures.

When vacancies happen in the representation of any State in the Senate, the executive authority of such State shall issue writs of election to fill such vacancies; *Provided,* That the legislature of any State may empower the executive thereof to make temporary appointments until the people fill the vacancies by election as the legislature may direct.

This amendment shall not be so construed as to affect the election or term of any Senator chosen before it becomes valid as a part of the Constitution.

## [ARTICLE XVIII.]

### (Adopted January 29, 1919)

**Section 1.** After one year from the ratification of this article the manufacture, sale, or transportation of intoxicating liquors within, the importation thereof into, or the exportation thereof from the United States and all territory subject to the jurisdiction thereof for beverage purposes is hereby prohibited.

**Section 2.** The Congress and the several States shall have concurrent power to enforce this article by appropriate legislation.

**Section 3.** This article shall be inoperative unless it shall have been ratified as an amendment to the Constitution by the legislatures of the several States, as provided in the Constitution, within seven years from the date of the submission hereof to the States by the Congress.

## [ARTICLE XIX.]

### (Adopted August 26, 1920)

The right of citizens of the United States to vote shall not be denied or abridged by the United States or by any State on account of sex.

Congress shall have power to enforce this article by appropriate legislation.

## [ARTICLE XX.]

### (Adopted January 23, 1933)

1. The terms of the President and Vice President shall end at noon on the 20th day of January, and the terms of Senators and Representatives at noon on the 3rd day of January, of the years in which such terms would have ended if this article had not been ratified; and the terms of their successors shall then begin.

2. The Congress shall assemble at least once in every year, and such meeting shall begin at noon on the 3rd day of January, unless they shall by law appoint a different day.

3. If, at the time fixed for the beginning of the term of the President, the President elect shall have died, the Vice President elect shall become President. If a President shall not have been chosen before the time fixed for the beginning of his term, or if the President elect shall have failed to qualify, then the Vice President elect shall act as President until a President shall have qualified; and the Congress may by law provide for the case wherein neither a President elect nor a Vice President elect shall have qualified, declaring who shall then act as President, or the manner in which one who is to act shall be selected, and such person shall act accordingly until a President or Vice President shall have qualified.

4. The Congress may by law provide for the case of the death of any of the persons from whom the House of Representatives may choose a President whenever the right of choice shall have devolved upon them, and for the case of the death of any of the persons from

whom the Senate may choose a Vice President whenever the right of choice shall have devolved upon them.

5. Sections 1 and 2 shall take effect on the 15th day of October following the ratification of this article (Oct., 1933).

6. This article shall be inoperative unless it shall have been ratified as an amendment to the Constitution by the Legislatures of three-fourths of the several States within seven years from the date of its submission.

## [ARTICLE XXI.]

### (Adopted December 5, 1933)

1. The eighteenth article of amendment to the Constitution of the United States is hereby repealed.

2. The transportation or importation into any State, Territory, or Possession of the United States for delivery or use therein of intoxicating liquors, in violation of the laws thereof, is hereby prohibited.

3. This article shall be inoperative unless it shall have been ratified as an amendment to the Constitution by conventions in the several States, as provided in the Constitution, within seven years from the date of the submission hereof to the States by the Congress.

## [ARTICLE XXII.]

### (Adopted February 27, 1951)

1. No person shall be elected to the office of the President more than twice, and no person who has held the office of President, or acted as President, for more than two years of a term to which some other person was elected President shall be elected to the office of the President more than once. But this Article shall not apply to any person holding the office of President when this Article was proposed by the Con-gress, and shall not prevent any person who may be holding the office of President, or acting as President, during the term within which this Article becomes operative from holding the office of President or acting as President during the remainder of such term.

2. This article shall be inoperative unless it shall have been ratified as an amendment to the Constitution by the Legislatures of three-fourths of the several States within seven years from the date of its submission to the States by the Congress.

## [ARTICLE XXIII.]

### (Adopted March 29, 1961)

1. The District constituting the seat of Government of the United States shall appoint in such manner as the Congress may direct:

A number of electors of President and Vice President equal to the whole number of Senators and Representatives in Congress to which the District would be entitled if it were a State, but in no event more than the least populous State; they shall be in addition to those appointed by the States, but they shall be considered, for the purposes of the election of President and Vice President, to be electors appointed by a State; and they shall meet in the District and perform such duties as provided by the twelfth article of amendment.

2. The Congress shall have power to enforce this article by appropriate legislation.

## [ARTICLE XXIV.]

### (Adopted January 23, 1964)

1. The right of citizens of the United States to vote in any primary or other election for President or Vice President, for electors for President or Vice President, or for Senator or Representative in Congress, shall not be denied or

abridged by the United States or any State by reason of failure to pay any poll tax or other tax.

2. The Congress shall have power to enforce this article by appropriate legislation.

## [ARTICLE XXV.]

### (Adopted February 10, 1965)

1. In case of the removal of the President from office or of his death or resignation, the Vice President shall become President.

2. Whenever there is a vacancy in the office of the Vice President, the President shall nominate a Vice President who shall take office upon confirmation by a majority vote of both houses of Congress.

3. Whenever the President transmits to the President pro tempore of the Senate and the Speaker of the House of Representatives his written declaration that he is unable to discharge the powers and duties of his office, and until he transmits to them a written declaration to the contrary, such powers and duties shall be discharged by the Vice President as Acting President.

4. Whenever the Vice President and a majority of either the principal officers of the executive departments or of such other body as Congress may by law provide, transmit to the President pro tempore of the Senate and the Speaker of the House of Representatives their written declaration that the President is unable to discharge the powers and duties of his office, the Vice President shall immediately assume the powers and duties of the office as Acting President.

Thereafter, when the President transmits to the President pro tempore of the Senate and the Speaker of the House of Representatives his written declaration that no inability exists, he shall resume the powers and duties of his office unless the Vice President and a majority of either the principal officers of the executive department or of such other body as Congress may by law provide, transmit within four days to the President pro tempore of the Senate and the Speaker of the House of Representatives their written declaration that the President is unable to discharge the powers and duties of his office. Thereupon Congress shall decide the issue, assembling within forty-eight hours for that purpose if not in session. If the Congress, within twenty-one days after receipt of the latter written declaration, or, if Congress is not in session, within twenty-one days after Congress is required to assemble, determines by two-thirds vote of both houses that the President is unable to discharge the powers and duties of his office, the Vice President shall continue to discharge the same as Acting President; otherwise, the President shall resume the powers and duties of his office.

## [ARTICLE XXVI.]

### (Adopted July 1, 1971)

1. The right of citizens of the United States, who are 18 years of age or older, to vote shall not be denied or abridged by the United States or any state on account of age.

2. The Congress shall have the power to enforce this article by appropriate legislation.

# Some Comments on the Constitution

"The basis of our political system is the right of the people to make and to alter their constitutions of government; but the Constitution which at any time exists, till changed by an explicit and authentic act of the whole people, is sacredly obligatory upon all. The very idea of the power and the right of the people to establish government presupposes the duty of every individual to obey the established government."
—GEORGE WASHINGTON

"The people made the Constitution, and the people can unmake it. It is the creature of their will, and lives only by their will. But this supreme and irresistible power to make or to unmake resides only in the whole body of the people; not in any subdivision of them. The attempt of any of the parts to exercise it is usurpation, and ought to be repelled by those to whom the people have delegated their power of repelling it."
—CHIEF JUSTICE JOHN MARSHALL

"There is no position which depends on clearer principles than that every act of a delegated authority, contrary to the tenor of the commission under which it is exercised, is void. No legislative act, therefore, contrary to the Constitution, can be valid. To deny this would be to affirm that the deputy is greater than his principal; that the servant is above his master; that the representatives of the people are superior to the people themselves; that men acting by virtue of power may do not only what their powers do not authorize, but what they forbid."
—ALEXANDER HAMILTON

"What are legislatures? Creatures of the Constitution; they owe their existence to the Constitution; it is their commission; and, therefore, all their acts must be comformable to it, or else they will be void. The Constitution is the work or will of the people themselves, in their original, sovereign, and unlimited capacity. Law is the work or will of the legislature in the derivative and subordinate capacity. The one is the work of the creator; the other of the creature. The Constitution fixes limits to the exercise of legislative authority and prescribes the orbit within which it must move."
—JUSTICE WILLIAM PATERSON

"To control the power and conduct of the legislature by an overruling Constitution, was an improvement in the science and practice of government reserved to the American States . . . . The truth is, that in our governments, the supreme, absolute and uncontrollable power remains in the people."
—JUSTICE JAMES WILSON

"To what purpose are powers limited, and to what purpose is that limitation committed to writing, if these limits may, at any time, be passed by those intended to be restrained? . . . It would be giving to the legislature a practical and real omnipotence with the same breath which professes to restrict their powers to narrow limits. It is prescribing limits, and declaring that those limits may be passed at pleasure. That it thus reduces to nothing what we have deemed the greatest improvement on political institutions, a written constitution, would of

itself be sufficient in America, where written constitutions have been viewed with so much reverence, for rejecting the construction."
—CHIEF JUSTICE JOHN MARSHALL

"The Constitution, therefore, being a fundamental law, . . . the judicial power, in the exercise of their authority, must take notice of it as the groundwork of that as well as of all other authority; and, as no article of the Constitution can be repealed by a legislature, which derives its whole power from it, it follows either that the fundamental unrepealable law must be obeyed, by the rejection of an act unwarranted by and inconsistent with it, or you must obey an act founded on an authority not given by the people, and to which, therefore, the people owe no obedience." —JUSTICE JAMES IREDELL

"Why does a judge swear to discharge his duties agreeably to the Constitution of the United States, if that Constitution forms no rule for his government—if it is closed upon him, and cannot be inspected by him? If such be the real state of things, this is worse than solemn mockery. To prescribe, or to take this oath becomes equally a crime. It is also not entirely unworthy of observation, that in declaring what shall be the supreme law of the land, the Constitution itself is first mentioned; and not the laws of the United States generally, but those only which shall be made in pursuance of the Constitution have that rank."
—CHIEF JUSTICE JOHN MARSHALL

"This government is acknowledged by all, to be one of enumerated powers. The principle, that it can exercise only the powers granted to it, would seem too apparent to have required to be enforced by all those arguments which its enlightened friends, while it was depending before the people, found it necessary to urge; that principle is now universally admitted."
—CHIEF JUSTICE SALMON CHASE

"Our history hitherto proves that the popular form (of government) is practicable, and that, with wisdom and knowledge, men may govern themselves; and the duty incumbent on us is to preserve the consistency of this cheering example, and take care that nothing may weaken its authority with the world. If, in our case, the representative system ultimately fail, popular government must be pronounced impossible. No combination of circumstances more favorable to the experiment can ever be expected to occur. The last hopes of mankind, therefore, rest with us; and if it should be proclaimed that our example had become an argument against the experiment, the knell of popular liberty would be sounded throughout the earth."
—DANIEL WEBSTER

"Let reverence of the law be breathed by every mother to the lisping babe that prattles on her lap; let it be taught in schools, seminaries, and colleges; let it be written in primers, spelling books, and almanacs; let it be preached from pulpits, and proclaimed in legislative halls, and enforced in courts of justice: let it become the political religion of the nation."
—ABRAHAM LINCOLN

# An Act for Establishing Religious Freedom

PASSED IN THE ASSEMBLY OF VIRGINIA (1785-1786)

Well aware that Almighty God hath created the mind free; that all attempts to influence it by temporal punishments or burdens, or by civil incapacitations, tend only to beget habits of hypocrisy and meanness, and are a departure from the plan of the Holy Author of our religion, who being Lord both of body and mind, yet chose not to propagate it by coercions on either, as was in his Almighty power to do;

That the impious presumption of legislators and rulers, civil as well as ecclesiastical, who, being themselves but fallible and uninspired men, have assumed dominion over the faith of others, setting up their own opinions and modes of thinking as the only true and infallible, and as such endeavoring to impose them on others, hath established and maintained false religions over the greatest part of the world, and through all time,

That to compel a man to furnish contributions of money for the propagation of opinions which he disbelieves, is sinful and tyrannical; that even the forcing of him to support this or that teacher of his own religious persuasion, is depriving him of the comfortable liberty of giving his contributions to the particular pastor whose morals he would make his pattern, and whose powers he feels most persuasive to righteousness, and is withdrawing from the ministry those temporal rewards, which proceeding from an approbation of their personal conduct, are an additional incitement to earnest and unremitting labors for the instruction of mankind;

That our civil rights have no dependence on our religious opinions, more than on our opinions in physics or geometry; that therefore the proscribing any citizen as unworthy the public confidence by laying upon him an incapacity of being called to offices of trust and emolument, unless he profess or renounce this or that religious opinion, is depriving him injuriously of those privileges and advantages to which in common with his fellow citizens he has a natural right;

That it tends also to corrupt the principles of that very religion it is meant to encourage, by bribing, with a monopoly of worldly honors and emoluments, those who will externally profess and conform to it; that though indeed these are criminal who do not withstand such temptation, yet neither are those innocent who lay the bait in their way;

That to suffer the civil magistrate to intrude his powers into the field of opinion and to restrain the profession or propagation of principles, on supposition of their ill tendency, is a dangerous fallacy, which at once destroys all religious liberty, because he being of course judge of that tendency will make his opinions the rule of judgment, and approve or condemn the sentiments of others only as they shall square with or differ from his own;

That it is time enough for the rightful purposes of civil government for its officers to interfere when principles break out into overt acts against peace and good order; and finally, that truth is great and will prevail if left to herself; that she is the proper sufficient antagonist to error, and has nothing to fear from the conflict, unless by human interposition disarmed of her natural weapons, free argument and debate; errors ceasing to be dangerous when it is permitted freely to contradict them;

We, the General Assembly, do enact, That no man shall be compelled to frequent or support any religious worship, place or ministry whatsoever, nor shall be enforced, restrained, molested, or burdened in his body or goods, nor shall otherwise suffer on account of his religious opinions or belief; but that all men shall be free to profess and by argument to maintain their opinions in matters of religion, and that the same shall in no wise diminish, enlarge, or effect their civil capacities.

And though we well know that this Assembly, elected by the people for the ordinary purposes of legislation only, have no power to restrain the acts of succeeding assemblies, constituted with power equal to our own, and that therefore to declare this act irrevocable would be of no effect in law, yet we are free to declare, and do declare, that the rights hereby asserted are of the natural rights of mankind, and that if any act shall be hereafter passed to repeal the present or to narrow its operation, such act will be an infringement of natural right.*

---

* Reprinted with permission. *Church and State Magazine.* © 1985.

# Human Rights and Christian Love
# By Former President Jimmy Carter

The Bible tells us to search for wisdom, to search for truth, to search for things that are permanent, that never change. The Bible tells us that we can find security in our religious beliefs. And, we can also find a purpose in life. While these kinds of characteristics, or attitudes, or treasures, or whatever you want to call them, are part of the result of a deep religious faith, they are the characteristics, obviously, that all of us would like to have in our public officials. The president of a college, the mayor of a city, the governor of a state, certainly the President of the United States or a member of Congress should have these characteristics (truth, security, a purpose, inspiration, and wisdom).

I have never found an incompatibility between my duties as a Christian and my duties as a governor or a President. I was sworn before God on Inauguration Day to obey and to preserve the Constitution of the United States and the laws of our nation. And I kept that oath. I tried to shape the principles, and morals, and standards, and even laws of our country, in a way that was beneficial to the people of this nation.

The highest calling of a Christian is to exhibit love in one's life. Jesus' disciples were always wondering about God the Father and on more than two occasions Christ gave them some clear descriptions which still stick in our minds.

What Christ was talking about was *agape* love, sacrificial love, love for another person without getting anything in return. Love for another person in a sacrificial way. Love for another person without even expecting to be loved back. Love for a person who doesn't deserve to be loved. That kind of love is the perfect love that God has for us, and that Christ had for those around him. On the cross itself, Jesus said, "Forgive them Father, for they know not what they do." So that sacrificial love, to oversimplify its meaning, is the highest possible calling for a human being.

**A great nation should be known as a champion of human rights.** This is not apple pie, and motherhood, and waving the flag on the Fourth of July. Human rights is an issue that cuts like a razor blade. It's difficult. It opens up wounds among those who are oppressors. Sometimes it creates a strain between us and our allies, particularly if our allies are oppressing their own people. But human rights need to

This selection is extracted from "Religion and American Foreign Policy," a lecture given by Former President Jimmy Carter, inaugurating the Messiah College Annual Lectures on Religion and Society, Messiah College, Grantham, Pennsylvania, February 18, 1986. Used by permission. The full text of this lecture appeared in the April 1986 issue of *The Bridge,* published by Messiah College, Grantham, PA 17927.

be protected, and preserved, and enhanced. In some parts of the world this is the number one burning issue. I think and hope that the policy that we followed while I was in the White House will keep human rights in the forefront of people's minds.

Well, let me say that although a nation can't measure up to the high standards of an individual human being, a nation's ability to achieve justice is dependent upon individual American willingness to achieve *agape* love. And if we lower our own individual standards as citizens of a democratic government or nation, then our nation's standards in foreign policy will inevitably be lowered.

Our nation depends on you and on me as private citizens. Because the higher the standards that we set to implement our own heartfelt beliefs—if we are Christians, our Christian beliefs—into the social structure of our nation, then the closer our nation's policies will be to our own.

If you are concerned about human rights, if you are concerned about hunger in Africa, if you are concerned about democracy or freedom, if you are concerned about environmental quality, if you are concerned about nuclear weapons, it is good to put some time on the subject. Study it, ask your professors to explain the intricacies of it. You won't find it a waste of time, because it is an extremely exciting and challenging thing to try to master a complicated subject. Maybe the Middle East, maybe Central America, maybe just Nicaragua, just El Salvador. Learn the names of those who participate. Try to understand both sides' views. And then, as you hear politicians make statements that are contrary to the facts, let your voice be heard.

Don't forget that one person in a democracy can make a difference. Each person can help shape our nation's foreign policy and domestic policy to be compatible with our deepest and most heartfelt beliefs.

# Dr. Halverson Answers Questions From the Dallas Workshop, Presbyterian Congress on Renewal, 1985

**Question:** In light of your comments on inputs in public policy, I wonder if you would comment on the wisdom of the Presbyterian Church denomination taking public positions in every issue that is present in the world today and, in that light, whether you feel that the denomination has the need for a paid Washington office to influence public policy in Washington?

**Answer:** I wanted to quote your father earlier and forgot. Let me quote his father first before I repeat the question. When I was in seminary, Duncan's father was the president, and to me, the greatest Protestant evangelical I've ever known. He used to say over and over again, "Whatever you make the issue, you make the idol." [Someone in the audience asked who his father was.] John A. Mackay, president of Princeton Seminary. Listen, it's Christ who unites us and if I allow an issue to divide us, then I'm making that issue more important than Jesus Christ. That issue is stronger in my life than Jesus Christ Himself is, because he who unites loses to an issue that divides. That's why one issue—voting—is not particularly good.

The question was—How do I feel about the Presbyterian denomination taking positions or stands concerning these issues? Well, I think my first answer to that, Duncan, is that it's inevitable. I've come to believe that bureaucracy is endemic in original sin. And I think that

that's what Babel is all about. I really think that that's what God saw in Babel in Genesis 11. Institutions take on a kind of self-identity that has absolutely no connection with the people that are a part of that institution. In this sense, when a denomination takes a position like that, it probably will not faithfully represent the people that it proposes to represent. In that respect I think it's wrong; I do think it's inevitable. I think these institutions are with us to stay.

Walter Judd, Member of Congress from Minnesota, used to talk about evangelism by mimeograph. He was referring to all the pressures and pronouncements he got, especially from church institutions, that had been mimeographed and sent to Members of Congress. So I think they're heard, but I don't think they impact public policy as much as we think they do.

I was reading an article by John Newhouse—he's the man who wrote *The Naked Public Square*—coming on the plane yesterday. I heard him in a White House briefing not so long ago and he was absolutely fantastic. His thesis is that if the public square is naked, evil things will occupy it, if we do not see that good things are there. I'm paraphrasing it, but that's the idea, and of course he's arguing that religion needs to be in the public square. Religion in the broadest sense and so on. I know this, that he

---

Above is the tape transcript of the questions and answers (by Dr. Richard C. Halverson) from the Dallas Workshop, Presbyterian Congress on Renewal.

feels that the Congress and all public officials need to know what the Church and the churches feel about things. The problem is, do they really represent the people they say they represent? Is that an adequate response?

**Question:** You mentioned a couple times about voting responsibly, the bewaring of the press and some of those kinds of things. Do you have any suggestions or comments as to good ways to secure information that doesn't have this slant one way or the other? Maybe that's asking the impossible.

**Answer:** Yes, I think this is possible, especially with members of Congress because they represent a relatively small group of people. But it would be easier to know the candidates for your district in the Congress or for the candidates for the city council, or the county supervisors, or the mayor, to the extent that you can know that candidate personally. You'd learn this from the friends of the candidate. You don't believe everything the candidate says, ever, because much political oratory is rhetoric and most people understand that and know that. If a candidate would really come down where the rubber meets the road in his campaign speeches, he probably wouldn't get anywhere, especially now with television. But I would say, first of all, to do everything you can to get to know your candidate and his or her qualifications on the basis of personal contacts, either yours or other people who know them. And then contact them to the extent that you can—visit them, talk to them on the phone, write letters and get answers, and so on. Is that an adequate answer?

**Question:** Yes. It seemed like, to me, that you were saying the character of the person is a very crucial aspect involving the issues and it seems that there is a distortion there of what I could present, at especially the national level, of that character. And that's what I'm trying to get a hold of, is how do I get a hold of this national character?

**Answer:** If they've been in public life, the experience they've had, what their image is in public life—and I don't mean image in the shallow sense, like a PR matter—but what they really have been like in public life, in local office, for example. And whether they can be trusted, what their family life is like. What their private life, to the extent that you can learn it, is like. What they are like as a husband and a father and a neighbor and as many things as you can learn to know whether or not this person has credibility and integrity. I know that it's not easy, but that's the point that I'm making. Vote for somebody that his integrity, even if you think he may not always vote the way you'd like.

**Question:** I just wanted to check out something that you said earlier. I know that there is strong substantiation for our form of government biblically; are you implying that the American system is the system which is advocated in Scripture, are you absolutizing it, or do you recognize that there might be other forms of government equally biblical?

**Answer:** Well, I think that the true biblical form of government is a benevolent monarchy. We have a King of kings and Lord of lords, and someday we're going to enjoy that Kingdom with Him. We ought to begin enjoying it right now. Is the American form of government the biblical form of government? No, I don't think that's true. I do think that the democratic system, because of human sin, is the most nearly right in terms of what we now call pluralism. I think of it as the diversity of human nature. It is the system which honors that diversity most and provides for it and respects it, serves it and so on in a way others don't.

**Question:** You mentioned your feelings of privacy of the public vote. Do you see any danger in exit polling, or is that kind of what you said about voting your own conscience or whatever, and having it be a private vote?

**Answer:** I think that the greatest danger of exit polling, which especially was illustrated four years ago, is when they let you know how it's gone, or assuming it's going a certain way even before your polls open. Exit polling is looked on much differently when you're on the East Coast than it is when you're on the West Coast. But I think that exit polling ought to be done very, very cautiously.

**Question:** I want to ask, how many Senators that you know, of the 100 that are there, are people who do profess to be Christians, have expressed that to you as a major consideration of their public policy considerations, and is there a breakdown in Republicans, Democrats, more of one than the other?

**Answer:** The Question is—Are there members of Congress, and are they evenly or unevenly divided, who are men and women of Christian character? Am I putting it pretty much the way you asked it?

I've brought this book cover along because I want to recommend it. This was published a year ago last November. It's called *Religion on Capitol Hill: Myths and Realities.* This book was published by Search, Inc., which is a professional polling organization. This is a survey that was made of Congress and its religious life at a very profoundly deep level. They didn't just want off-the-top-of-the-head comments about one being an Episcopalian or a Presbyterian, or Protestant, Catholic or Jew, etc.; They wanted to provoke from the members of Congress they interview their deepest feelings about religion and about their commitment. They report that in this book. I recommend it.

Incidentally, the myths and realities—here are the myths that they explode in that book: Is Congress a hotbed of secular humanism, agnosticism and atheism? The answer is no, but there is an assumption that it is by many. Are members of Congress less religious than the people they serve? The answer is no; as a matter of fact, they are more religious, according to the survey. Are political conservatives more religious than political liberals? Again the answer is no, though the assumption is the other way. Do religious beliefs and values have a significant impact on how members vote on issues? The answer to that is they have significant impact, but not in a kind of simplistic way that you and I might expect. They really cover that in depth in the book. Are evangelical Christians in Congress a united conservative political force? The answer is no. Is it true that members who affirm basic Christian fundamentals adopt the politically conservative position of the new Christian right, while members who are atheists or secular humanist are politically liberal?

The first fact is there are no atheists in Congress on the base of that survey. A little bit of agnosticism, but very little. Every Member of Congress, according to the survey, believes in God, 40 percent of the Congress profess faith in Christ as Saviour and Lord. One of the conclusions that they reached is that the religious commitment of men and women in Congress is greater than the people they represent in private life. So that's a lot better answer.

Now I have my own ideas about that, but there's nothing that I've learned in this that goes against my own experience, I don't think that there are more Republicans who are Christian than Democrats, or Republicans are Christian, Democrats are not. That really is a myth. Some of the most godly men and women I know are on the Democratic side of the aisle in the Senate. So I think that you get your best answer from this.

**Question:** I noticed in the description of the workshop that you referred to our form of government as a republic, rather than as a democracy, and I wondered if that was intentional and whether Congress is aware of the growing constitutional movement, the patriot groups, and what you think?

**Answer:** No, that certainly wasn't intentional. I wasn't trying to make a point. I use the word republic as a synonym for nation governed by representation. To me, it is a republic. The political process by which we operate is a democracy or democratic. But I certainly wasn't trying to make a point in saying that.

**Question:** Is Congress aware of the patriot groups and the constitutional movements and so forth that are growing in number in various states?

**Answer:** I would guess that they are. There is a—I don't want to say a fear, because I don't think that's a good word—but there is a concern about a movement for another constitutional convention. The reason for that is the fear that that would open the door in this day of pluralism to all kinds of issues that would preoccupy a constitutional convention. It wouldn't get right at the thing; for example, voluntary school prayer, or abortion, these issues. That is one of the concerns, that it wouldn't be able to deal with just those, it would open the door to a complete change of our Constitution. By the way, in that context, let me tell you that one of the thrilling things to me since I've been in Washington, and especially since I've been in the Senate, is the tremendous concern to be constitutional. It's absolutely amazing to hear these debates and the argument as to whether or not this is constitutional. That's a document that was written 200 years ago, and we're not only trying to live by it, but it's taken very, very seriously by the leadership of our nation.

**Question:** You have made several references to the earnest Christian faith of people on different sides of great issues that we're talking about. Obviously that's the case in the Church at large also. Could you share some of your own experience about what kinds of things might have been helpful in their communicating with each other as Christians on the basis of a biblical faith, to see whether there is common ground or negotiating, or has there been any help along that line? I worked for the state government for these past two years in Sacramento and I'm really interested in what possible structures may assist in dialogue, like someone has mentioned The C.S. Lewis Institute, but I don't know anything about it.

**Answer:** The question is—In the light of the differences among those who profess faith in Christ, or the differences among the churches concerning many, if not most of the issues that the Congress faces or the legislative bodies face, is there any communication between them; are there efforts made to talk these things through?

When I listened to the debate on abortion, and I probably am opening the door to some real problems for myself now, so let me say first of all that before I left Fourth Presbyterian Church as its pastor, we had all of the Schaeffer films on abortion. And we had long discussions about them and I am unalterably opposed to abortion. I think it's a sick, awful evil and there ought to be a law against it like there is a law against murder and so on. But in the course of the debate, I spoke with one senator, who shall remain anonymous, for whom the issue was a deep and heavy struggle with agony. The senator was unalterably opposed to abortion, but also unalterably opposed to anything that's going to rob us, that's going to make inroads on liberty. Now I don't agree with that, mind you, but as I listened to that debate, this is what I heard, this tremendous concern about liberty as well as life.

I came out of that debate trying to urge pro-life people to listen to those for whom liberty was such an important issue, that the way might be open for dialogue. Obviously I was misunderstood, for I received a great deal of mail from people trying to convince me to be anti-abortion. But what I was saying was, I believe that we who are pro-life would be in a much greater position to communicate what we really believe with those who are called pro-choice; not all of them, of course, but for those who take liberty seriously on the basis of the Constitution. If we'd listen to them, we might have an opportunity to talk to them abut what we see as the horror of abortion. But I didn't feel that was ever heard.

So my answer really is that I feel that there isn't a great deal of communication in the Church between those who have differences about most of these issues. We just believe and shout and we don't listen to the other person, not simply to be convinced by them, but in order that we might, having heard them, share with them our deepest convictions about whatever the issue is. So I think there is very little of that and there ought to be more. We need to listen.

**Question:** How about at the prayer breakfasts? Have you accomplished some of that there?

**Answer:** I think that happens, yes; not as it ought to happen though. But incidentally, there are many little groups in Congress who are opposite on many of these issues, but in Christ they're united in love and they discuss these things a great deal in that context.

**Question:** I want to make a comment rather than ask a question and it refers to the point on the national church's involvement in policy statement and so forth. And I think I sense probably throughout the whole Congress that there will be some sentiment against the positions of the national church. I think that one of the things that we need to realize is that, at least as far as I can perceive, all sources of information are suspect, whether they are from the government or special interest groups or whatever. And in our search for truth we need to listen to as many voices as possible, and so I rely on our national church's information and policy statements, at least as the source of information that I can measure other statements which are at least equally suspect. So I think before we write off our national church and its position, we ought to realize that it is a source of information from people who are, at least at face value, practicing Christians similar to our frame of reference. So, we ought to at least listen and appreciate that source of information rather than to assume that they ought not be speaking. I appreciate what our national church does from a political standpoint, because it is a source of information from which can evolve my conclusion.

**Answer:** Thank you for saying that, and it must be said too, I think, that none of these issues are off the top of the head by a national church. They have committees that really do some deep research and study. The important question is, do they really represent their constituency or don't they? Is that judgment the judgment of an elite?

Now most of the things we read, we can assume most of the things we get through the press and the media, especially from the top men and women, are on the basis of an elite who disagree completely with almost everything that we believe in. About 85 percent of this journalistic elite, the Gallup poll indicated, never go to church, do not believe in God and the Bible. They hold no sense of absolute morality. So I think we need to realize that they don't even represent the press, for that matter. But to me that's the only thing to be concerned about. I think we need to take all the advantage we can out of those sources, but not assume that they represent their constituency.

**Question:** I've always understood that the national church speaks to the church and not for the church. I'm interested in my own role as a pastor in that sense, and I realize that I may express opinions and preaching from the Bible that do not represent the people to whom I'm preaching, but I have a responsibility to speak what I believe to be God's Word to the church, related to the various issues with which we're confronted. What I'd like to hear you talk about is how you, as a pastor, can keep the role of a preacher as addressing political, social, economic issues that so often divide people, how do you address those from the pulpit and what is our responsibility in that regard?

**Answer:** There's a long question here—"How does a pastor, how do I as a pastor, address these issues? Well, there's a long answer to that; I'll try to really make it brief. Number one, I was pastor in Washington for 23 years. Now you realize when you have the pulpit in Washington, D.C., every issue that's national or regional or international is a local issue in Washington, D.C. There are on the average three protests a day in Washington, D.C. Some of them are relatively small, some of them are huge, which is part of the answer. You've got a platform in a city where anything that is happening anywhere in the world is local news and the whole front page of the Washington papers reflects this. As a matter of fact, when I first went back to Los Angeles where I came from in 1956 and looked at the Los Angeles paper, it seemed like a county paper that I remembered from my days in North Dakota. Now that's an exaggeration, of course. But I felt it was really parochial as I read the front page of the Los Angeles papers.

My own experience is that, first of all, the pulpit is committed to the exposition of the Word of God, not to the discussion of issues. I planned my sermons a year ahead. I was taught that by Dr. Blackwood at Princeton Seminary and it was the most important course perhaps I had. I planned a year's preaching faithfully every single year so that when I met with the officers in a fall retreat I could tell them what I was going to be preaching about every Sunday for the following year.

Now that didn't mean that I was locked in—the Holy Spirit could lead differently. But the amazing thing to me was, as I kept faith with the whole counsel of God, that is not just preaching on favorite texts, and was sensitive to the needs of the people to whom Christ had sent me to serve as pastor, and aware of the near and far environment in which God had planted this congregation, it was amazing the way, Sunday after Sunday, expository messages, which had been thought about and prayed about and planned long before, were relevant to the issues at hand. It never seemed necessary to lift an issue up and say, "Today I'm going to talk about this issue." I went through the whole Civil Rights Movement and the Vietnam War during my pastorate in Washington. My experience indicates that when you're faithful to the Scriptures, you are relevant to the issues as they arise. The most dramatic of those was during the whole Watergate time, how Sunday after Sunday the messages, though I knew nothing about Watergate obviously when I planned them, it was amazing how they were relevant to the Watergate situation as it developed in the city.

**Question:** I really resonated to what you were saying about our system of representing government of the people and not surrendering our sovereignty. But I'm profoundly concerned about how we be sure not to surrender our sovereignty as Presbyterians. I value very much the Declaration of the General Assembly, not that I always agree with them, but that is a process by which my vote as an individual is reflected in influencing national policy. Now somebody has already said that before, but I'm wondering, can you give us some particular ideas of how we as members of a church that prides itself on being a representative of democracy can make our church more reflective of our grass roots, the consensus on issues, if there is a consensus?

**Answer:** Let me say very simply, in answer to that question, how can we find a consensus or how can we exercise our sovereignty more as members of a denomination? Very simply, I'm deeply convinced that what we're doing here in Dallas these three days is probably as necessary as anything that we do as a church. I have tremendous expectation, I'm very excited that it is happening, especially since I heard that sermon just before we came down here, but also Dale Bruner's exegesis earlier than that. I am expecting God to touch us.

Now I'm not thinking of something spectacular or dramatic, but I'm asking God to touch us in some quiet way. If it's dramatic, so let it be, but I don't demand that. I expect God to touch us as we are here in a way that benevolently infects the whole body—not just the Presbyterian Church, but all of the churches around us—because we believe in a connectional church. I'm expecting and praying that God will do something here that will touch every one of us so that we will return like a benevolent infection to our local congregations.

I connected the first statement, "We hold these truths to be self-evident that all men are created equal," with the last statement of those two sentences, "That the government receives its just powers but from the consent of the governed," and suggesting those two were fundamental; but I think the sovereignty of the people is absolutely dependent upon their submission to the sovereignty of God. In other words, when God is Lord, then the people are qualified to manage and control their environment. When God is not Lord, then they are going to become the victims of their environment, whether it's physical, political, social, or whatever else. That's fundamental, so we give God His place in our lives, in our church—and I'm not assuming that we haven't—but I think that's what revival, renewal or awakening is all about, so I have this hope.

Let me close by a statement that's on the walls of the Jefferson Memorial in Washington, D.C. As you enter the memorial from the Tidal Basin, on the right hand wall are those two sentences from the Declaration of Independence, which I quoted earlier. As you go out, there is another long paragraph of Thomas Jefferson's. Incidentally, John Newhouse quoted this in his book *The Naked Public Square*. Jefferson stated a categorical statement and then asked a question. The categorical statement is this: "God, who gave us life, gave us liberty." Then the question: "Can those liberties be sustained if we abandon the God who gave them?" I think that's a fair question, and it is as relevant as any question we face in our nation today. God bless you. Thanks so much for the privilege, and remember my fallibility.

# Books Recommended For Reading and Reference

**Story, Commentaries on the Constitution.** (A comprehensive exposition of the Constitution, not only on its technical and legal side, but from the point of view of history and for its popular understanding, by Joseph Story, a former Justice of the Supreme Court.)

**The Federalist.** (A series of papers, written in explanation and defense of the Constitution, at the time when it was before the States for adoption, by Alexander Hamilton and James Madison.)

**Madison's Journal of the Convention.** (Edited by Gaillard Hunt.) (A contemporary record of the doings and debates of the Convention which framed the Constitution, by James Madison, called the "Father of the Constitution.")

**Farrand, The Framing of the Constitution.** (A popular account of the formation of the Constitution, by Professor Max Farrand of Yale.)

**Bartlett, Handy Book of American Government.** (A brief and popular description of the institutions and operations of the government of the United States, following the order of the Constitution.)

**Hill, The People's Government.** (An exposition of the system of constitutional government in the United States, with special reference to the fundamental rights of individuals, the supremacy of law, and the relation of the citizen to the state, by David Jayne Hill.)

**Hill, Americanism: What It Is.** (An account of those principles and features of our system of government which make "Americanism" a distinctive creed and institution, with a study of the rights, duties and responsibilities of American citizenship. By David Jayne Hill.)

**Baker, Fundamental Law of American Constitution.** (A series of lectures, discussing the principles and practice of American constitutional government in the light of history and the decisions of the courts. In three volumes.)

**Bryce, The American Commonwealth.** (A comprehensive but popular description of the organization and working of government in the United States and the States, and of American political institutions, by James Bryce, now Viscount Bryce, former British ambassador to the United States.)

**Lieber, Civil Liberty and Self Government.** (An account of the origins and establishment of the principles of civil and political liberty under constitutional government, with a valuable appendix of original documents. By Francis Lieber.)

**Lodge, The Democracy of the Constitution.** (Essays and addresses on important aspects of the Constitution. By United States Senator Henry Cabot Lodge.)

**Sutherland, Constitutional Power and World Affairs.** (Lectures on the extent and limitation of the powers conferred by the Constitution as affecting war and the making of treaties. By Associate Justice George Sutherland.)

**Black, The Relation of the Executive Power to Legislation.** (An essay on the growth and development of the executive power in its relation to the initiation and enactment of the laws. By Henry Campbell Black, Editor of The Constitutional Review.)

**The Constitutional Review.** (A quarterly magazine, advocating the maintenance of constitutional government and recording its progress at home and abroad.)

# Pamphlets

Relating to the Constitution or the principles of constitutional government, which will be furnished on request by THE NATIONAL ASSOCIATION FOR CONSTITUTIONAL GOVERNMENT, 716 Colorado Building, Washington, D.C.

"Representative Government and the Common Law," by Emmet O'Neal, former Governor of Alabama.

"How the Constitution Saved the Revolution," by Gaillard Hunt.

"What the Constitution Does for the Citizen," by Henry A. Wise Wood.

"The Americanism of the Constitution of the United States," by Judge William W. Morrow, U.S. Circuit Court of Appeals.

"Experiments in Government," "The Essentials of the Constitution," (price 10 cents each), by former Senator Elihu Root.

"Reactionary Tendencies of Radicalism," by Professor Wm. H. Doughty, Jr., of Williams College.

# Notes

1. From "Washington Whispers," *U.S. News & World Report,* September 1, 1986. Copyright, 1986, *U.S. News & World Report.* Used by permission.

2. Romauld Spasowski, *The Liberation of One* (San Diego, CA: Harcourt Brace Javonavich, Inc., 1986).

3. Senator Spark Matsunaga, Congressional Record Vol. 132 No. 145, pages S17229, S17230. Public domain.

4. From "Washington Whispers," *U.S. News & World Report,* August 25, 1986. Copyright, 1986, *U.S. News & World Report.* Used by permission.

5. "The Selling of the Candidates," *U.S. News & World Report,* September 8, 1986, Copyright, 1986, *U.S. News & World Report.* Used by permission.

6. Ibid.

7. Thomas Jefferson. Public domain.

8. Anthony Campollo, *Partly Right* (Word, Inc., 1985). Used by permission.

9. Rev. Doctor Allan Bosack. Public domain.

10. Thomas Jefferson. Public domain.

11. Malcolm Muggeridge. Public domain.

12. "A Modicum of Trust" by Mortimer B. Zuckerman, *U.S. News & World Report,* September 22, 1986. Copyright, 1986, *U.S. News & World Report.* Used by permission.

13. Abraham Lincoln. Public domain.

14. Eugene Thomas Long, *God, Secularization and History* (University of South Carolina Press). Used by permission.

15. "The Illusion of Permanence" by David Lawrence, *U.S. News & World Report,* May 25, 1956. Copyright, 1956, *U.S. News & World Report.* Used by permission.

16. Douglas MacArthur. Public domain.

17. Thomas Jefferson. Public domain.

18. Dennis F. Kinlaw, Permission to reprint granted.